Cover Image Credit/Copyright Attribution: IIIerlok_Xolms/Shutterstock

Integrating SSR and SALW Programming

Mark Sedra and Geoff Burt

Published by
Ubiquity Press Ltd.
6 Osborn Street, Unit 2N
London E1 6TD

First published 2016
Transferred to Ubiquity Press 2018

Editors: Heiner Hänggi & Albrecht Schnabel
Associate editor: Fairlie Chappuis
Editorial assistance: Kathrin Reed
Copy editor: Cherry Ekins

DOI: https://doi.org/10.5334/bca

This book was originally published by the Geneva Centre for the Democratic Control of Armed Forces (DCAF), an international foundation whose mission is to assist the international community in pursuing good governance and reform of the security sector. The title transferred to Ubiquity Press when the series moved to an open access platform. The full text of this book was peer reviewed according to the original publisher's policy at the time. The original ISBN for this title was 978-92-9222-414-1.

SSR Papers is a flagship DCAF publication series intended to contribute innovative thinking on important themes and approaches relating to security sector reform (SSR) in the broader context of security sector governance (SSG). Papers provide original and provocative analysis on topics that are directly linked to the challenges of a governance-driven security sector reform agenda. SSR Papers are intended for researchers, policy-makers and practitioners involved in this field.

The views expressed are those of the author(s) alone and do not in any way reflect the views of the institutions referred to or represented within this paper.

Contents

Introduction

Security sector reform (SSR) and small arms and light weapons (SALW) reduction and control programmes have become standard features of contemporary peacebuilding and statebuilding processes. Much of the literature on peacebuilding and statebuilding draws explicit linkages between the two areas, which it regards as interdependent and mutually enabling. The implementation of SALW reduction and control programmes in fragile, failed and conflict-affected states (FFCAS) is characteristically touted as a critical step towards achieving one of the overarching goals of SSR: the consolidation of a state monopoly over the legitimate use of coercive force. After all, as one United Nations (UN) report explains:

> An SALW programme is not only a matter of weapons, but the creation of an environment where the government can govern, where the police and armed forces can be trusted, where different communities can live alongside each other and where sustainable development can take place in a secure environment.[1]

Conversely, SSR in a transition country provides a vital foundation for SALW programming. This is because it both creates the governance capacity needed to enforce SALW control regimes and encourages communities to have enough trust in the state's capacity for non-partisan public protection to consider surrendering their personal weapons. In contexts of conflict and state fragility, general populations and non-state armed groups alike would be reluctant to relinquish their arms without a guarantee that local security forces will provide for their security equitably, effectively and in line with the rule of law. Hence, there is a need for a robust SSR agenda. As Donald and Olonisakin affirm:

> [D]emand for small arms is a function primarily of the perception of threat. Once a state's citizens feel they have a share in a responsive political process, and that the security apparatus is likely to stick to what it's supposed to, genuine security – and thus limited demand – are likely to follow.[2]

Most existing international policy and programmatic frameworks for democratic transitions in FFCAS – whether formulated by donor states, recipient governments or intergovernmental organizations – recognize linkages between SSR and SALW programming. However, as is often the case in complex transition environments, theory has characteristically failed to translate into practice. In numerous contexts SALW reduction and control activities have been advanced autonomously of the SSR agenda, and vice versa. The failure to exploit synergies between SSR and SALW programming can not only have the effect of obstructing peacebuilding processes, but also become a driver of instability in its own right. Accordingly, this paper seeks to identify some of the factors that have prevented the harmonization and coordination of SSR and SALW programmes in FFCAS, and recommend approaches to bolster the integration of the two areas. The paper intends to show how the integration of SSR and SALW programming in FFCAS can greatly improve their mutual prospects for success, allowing peacebuilders and statebuilders to maximize scarce resources. Greater integration at the micro field level, however, requires more integrated strategies and institutional mechanisms at macro international and national levels, which will require substantial change in the *modus operandi* of many key SSR and SALW stakeholders.

Policymakers and practitioners are keenly aware that ineffective, repressive and corrupt state security sectors can increase demand for guns among civilian populations.[3] The UN outlines the varied causal links between a weak security sector and increased demand for SALW:

> Weak security sectors ... tend to be highly politicized. This leads to a lack of accountability, increased corruption, lack of coordination, limited

professional competence and interagency rivalries. This in turn can lead to a security vacuum that may be filled by warring factions or organized criminal groups, resulting in greater insecurity, which leads to an increase in the demand for and use of weapons by the community, as the demand for weapons is directly related to the perception of threat. The laws of supply and demand are as equally valid for weapons as anything else, and the lack of a credible security sector makes the supply of weapons to meet this demand relatively easy.[4]

Conversely, the idea that SALW proliferation can lead to the breakdown of state order and the erosion of the security sector's ability to safeguard communities and uphold the rule of law is well understood.[5] However, SSR and SALW field missions have more often than not failed to actualize this intrinsic link explicitly in their programming. In countries where this critical connection has informed programme strategies, such as Albania and Malawi, notable successes in community violence reduction and peacebuilding have been achieved. In cases where cross-programme synergies have not been nurtured, such as in Afghanistan and the Democratic Republic of the Congo (DRC), major setbacks have been experienced. It has become all too clear in these contexts that the impact of even well-constructed SALW reduction and control efforts will prove to be short-lived if not accompanied by reforms in the security sector.

The mixed record of SSR in FFCAS, marked by a lack of clear successes since the concept's emergence at the end of the Cold War, has contributed to the policy–practice divide characterizing the SSR–SALW relationship.[6] The SSR policy model clearly advocates robust coordination with SALW reduction and control activities, but this has not delivered concrete programmatic connections on the ground. In recent years the drift of many SSR programmes towards a "train-and-equip" approach reminiscent of the Cold War era has dampened enthusiasm for SSR–SALW integration. Quite to the contrary, this trend has emphasized the rearmament of partner governments rather than the disarmament and "right-sizing" of security institutions. In the era of the "war on terror", strengthening the coercive capacity of regimes at the front lines of counterterrorism operations has seemingly eclipsed the imperatives of SALW reduction and the strengthening of democratic security sector governance. Indeed, far from furthering programmatic integration, this train-and-equip approach has placed many SSR agendas at odds with SALW reduction and control programmes. It is against this challenging backdrop that the efficacy of existing strategies in SSR and SALW programming has been fundamentally critiqued and questioned, opening up space for new implementation approaches and methods. While the integration of SSR and SALW reduction and control programming in the field may not be a great innovation in normative terms, in practice it could represent a breakthrough. A new move to exploit the synergies between the two projects may bear significant fruit in improving their prospects to make decisive contributions to community violence reduction and peacebuilding.

Enhancing the integration of SSR and SALW reduction and control projects in FFCAS requires first and foremost renewed political will among major bilateral donors and international organizations, as well as their partner countries. The donors and international organizations must invest in this strategic reorientation, while their partner countries must accept a more holistic reform agenda that could challenge sacrosanct notions of national sovereignty. Indeed, one of the reasons why SSR and SALW reduction and control programmes have been advanced in silos is the reluctance of recipient governments to countenance sweeping programmes that simultaneously seek to reduce the coercive power of state and non-state actors and to transform state security institutions in line with democratic principles. The oft-contentious nature of SSR and SALW reduction and control programmes in volatile FFCAS has prompted both donors and recipients to advance them separately, reducing their perceived level of complexity, contentiousness and capacity for political disruption.

Quite apart from the political challenges, a concrete obstacle to SSR–SALW integration revolves around the day-to-day demands, often technical in nature, it involves in the field. It has proven difficult in practice to harmonize the strategies and agendas of the numerous domestic and international actors engaged in SSR and SALW reduction and control activities. Moreover, different actors and agencies, both foreign and domestic, often have different agendas on the ground. For instance, in the same context a UN body in concert with a local government agency could be seeking to advance disarmament at the same time as a bilateral donor in alliance with a government security institution is arming state and/or non-state actors to advance counterterrorism objectives. Such is the murkiness of contemporary peacebuilding and statebuilding environments. Garnering the necessary resources and political will to overcome these political and practical obstacles to integration has been vexing. Bridging the gulf between policy and practice may require reform and even reconceptualization of SSR and SALW models.

This paper has three sections. The first looks at the SSR–SALW connection conceptually, examining how the relationship is framed in policy and academic discourse. It pays special attention to how seminal international SSR guidance documents treat the relationship and how it is framed in key SALW agreements and protocols promulgated by the UN, the African Union (AU) and other multilateral bodies. It also maps the practical areas of SSR–SALW convergence and identifies some of the main disincentives for integration. The second section explores these interconnections in practice through analysis of six case-study countries: Malawi, Albania, Cambodia, El Salvador, the DRC and Afghanistan. When it comes to SSR–SALW integration and programme impacts, this diverse group, featuring varied ground-level conditions, contains cases of clear success, partial success and outright failure. By grouping the countries in these three outcome categories, the section can comparatively illustrate the benefits of integration. It wraps up with a brief synthesis of the case-study material, identifying common trends and lessons learned. The paper concludes with concrete recommendations on avenues to enable and strengthen the synergies between SSR and SALW programming. Taken together, the conceptual overview and comparative case-study analysis present a strong case for SSR–SALW integration as a means to enhance programmatic impacts in FFCAS.

Conceptualizing the SSR-SALW Relationship

SSR theory emphasizes the necessity of integrating SSR and SALW reduction and control programmes as part of a comprehensive security transition in FFCAS.[7] In practice, however, these programmes are typically advanced in isolation, supported by different external donors and domestic stakeholders, and often with different strategies and aims. Before exploring the SSR–SALW linkage as it has been outlined in conceptual and policy terms, it is important to define the two processes briefly. The Organisation for Economic Co-operation and Development's Development Assistance Committee (OECD-DAC) *Handbook on Security System Reform* defines SALW reduction and control programmes as encompassing the following key features:

- The development of laws, regulations and administrative procedures to exercise effective control over the production, export, import and transit of SALW.
- The development of institutional structures for policy guidance, research and monitoring.
- Activities to improve the management and security of stockpiles of SALW and related ammunition and explosives, particularly those held by the police, the military and other forces authorized by the state.

- The destruction of SALW and related ammunition and explosives that are deemed surplus to national security requirements.
- Public awareness campaigns on SALW and voluntary SALW collection and destruction programmes.
- The promotion of regional and subregional cooperation and information exchange to prevent, combat and eradicate the illicit trade in SALW across borders.[8]

It is important to emphasize the distinction between the two main pillars of SALW programming: reduction and control. The reduction pillar refers to disarmament and involves the "collection and destruction of weapons, sometimes combined with erecting barriers against acquisition of new weapons. It can be incremental, partial, or comprehensive."[9] Control, by contrast, "refers to regulations establishing ownership, limiting acquisition of certain quantities or types of weapons or ammunition, or restricting storage, transfer, and resale. Control does not aim to reduce weapons numbers, but rather to ensure greater safety of existing and future inventories."[10] The disarmament area can be further broken down into three components or types: civilian weapons collection and destruction, state disarmament and the disarmament of non-state armed groups.[11] All three types engage and even target the security sector in different ways.

In her 1999 speech in which she coined the term SSR, UK Secretary of State for International Development Clare Short explained that "one of the principal obstacles to progress in development and poverty reduction … is the existence of bloated, secretive, repressive, undemocratic and poorly structured security sectors in many developing countries".[12] Following Short's speech, the notion "that self-sustaining security depends upon the creation of a legitimate, democratically accountable and effective indigenous security sector" became, in the words of Bellamy, "a new aid paradigm".[13] It came to be accepted, as the UN's Integrated Technical Guidance Notes (ITGNs) on SSR affirm, that SSR can make an indispensible contribution "to international peace and security, sustainable development, and the enjoyment of human rights by all".[14]

The SSR concept assumes an expansive definition of the security sector, encompassing the security forces and the relevant civilian bodies needed to manage them; the state institutions which have a formal mandate to ensure the safety of the state and its citizens against acts of violence and coercion; and the elected and duly appointed civil authorities responsible for control and oversight of these institutions.[15] The objective of SSR "is to strengthen the ability of the sector as a whole and each of its individual parts to provide an accountable, equitable, effective, and rights respecting service".[16] As UN Secretary-General Ban Ki-moon stated in May 2014, "a professional and accountable security sector under the framework of the rule of law can strengthen public confidence in the State and provide the stability necessary for peacebuilding and development".[17] He went on to stress that the aim of SSR was a "collective goal" of the UN.[18] What makes the SSR model distinct from more conventional forms of security assistance – epitomized by train-and-equip programmes fixated solely on increasing the coercive capacity of security institutions – is its dedication to democratic norms of good governance and its expansive and holistic definition of the sector that looks beyond the hard security institutions of the state.[19]

The UN Security Council's first standing resolution on SSR (Resolution 2151, adopted in 2014)[20] reaffirmed the importance of SSR for "the consolidation of peace, and stability, promoting poverty reduction, rule of law and good governance, extending legitimate State authority, and preventing countries from relapsing into conflict".[21] It also reiterated "the centrality of national ownership ... informed by broader national political processes" and the imperative of "supporting 'sector-wide' initiatives that aim to enhance the governance and overall performance of the security sector".[22] Addressing a common criticism of SSR, the resolution emphasized that "SSR is not just a matter of technical support"[23] but requires the investment of political capital. The resolution demonstrated a new UN commitment to adopt a political approach to SSR processes; to enhance and expand partnerships with regional and bilateral SSR stakeholders; and to develop new training and capacity-building resources.

Paradoxically, the rapid institutionalization of SSR policy and practice in the international security and development communities has only been paralleled by its meagre success rate in the field. Perhaps the defining characteristic of the last decade of SSR implementation is a policy–practice gap.[24] The comprehensive model of SSR policy and practice, reflected in key documents like the 2007 OECD-DAC *Handbook on Security System Reform*, the UN Secretary-General's report on "Securing peace and development: The role of the United Nations in supporting security sector reform"[25] and the UN ITGNs, has rarely been actualized in practice, with its defining principles, such as the emphasis on good governance and democratic civilian control, characteristically underresourced or even ignored in many contexts. Even a cursory look at SSR implementation cases over the past decade shows a consistent pattern of underperformance when it comes to actualizing the defining norms and principles of the SSR model. As Egnell and Haldén explain, SSR programmes tended only to be "successful in countries where not only sovereign state structures of a 'Westphalian' type existed, but which also had civil societies, albeit in rudimentary forms, and where a clear notion of a common polity existed and was shared by major elites and power holders".[26] In most contemporary FFCAS, which at best could be referred to as "quasi-states"[27] in that they feature juridical sovereignty but lack the ability to furnish the public goods of modern states, SSR has been hard-pressed to drive desired change.

Intricately intertwined with SSR and SALW programmes in FFCAS is another critical device of peacebuilding and statebuilding: the disarmament, demobilization and reintegration (DDR) of former combatants. DDR represents a critical area of overlap and convergence for SSR and SALW reduction and control programmes. The OECD-DAC *Handbook on Security System Reform* recognizes that "SSR and DDR programmes need to be considered as part of a comprehensive security and justice development programme" and "implemented in close alignment".[28] By extension, "poor performance in one component of DDR can undermine SSR and SALW control", and vice versa.[29] As McFate explains, the "interrelated and mutually reinforcing" nature of DDR and SSR programmes means "they succeed or fail together and should be planned, resourced, implemented, and evaluated in a coordinated manner".[30]

DDR is a discrete project launched in the early stages of a security transition that aims to contribute to the consolidation of peace and stability by "removing weapons from the hands of combatants, taking the combatants out of military structures and helping them to integrate socially and economically into society".[31] DDR programmes are, as Karp suggests, "the most rigorously studied aspect of small arms disarmament" and "far and away the most visible and best funded".[32] DDR is firmly embedded in the lexicon and toolkit of peacebuilding and statebuilding for FFCAS.[33] By decommissioning armed groups and removing weapons from circulation, DDR programmes endeavour to create the security space and public trust to advance medium- and long-term reforms of the security sector. DDR programmers have not always recognized the interconnectivity between DDR and SSR programmes. However, recent iterations of DDR in places like the Central African Republic, Libya, Mali and Yemen have seen it reimagined as part of a dynamic political process "connected in complex ways to peace negotiations and robust peace operations, justice and security sector reform, and peace- and statebuilding".[34] In the eyes of Muggah and O'Donnell, "this new wave of DDR represents ... a move away from narrowly conceived stand-alone interventions toward activities that are purposefully connected to national development plans".[35]

As these definitions and descriptions show, SSR, SALW and DDR programmes share the same aims and conceptual underpinnings. They are all dedicated to reducing armed violence and consolidating peace and stability by fostering a monopoly over the use of coercive force. Hence, as the OECD-DAC *Handbook* recognizes, their fates are intertwined in FFCAS:

> The timing of programmes to reduce the number of weapons in civilian hands needs to be closely linked to how well DDR and SSR initiatives are progressing. People will be unwilling to surrender their weapons while they are still in danger from armed groups and in the absence of effective provision of security. Visible progress on police reform is often vital to increase the public's perceptions of security as a precursor to weapons collection programmes.[36]

In spite of this clear interconnectivity and even mutual dependence, the OECD-DAC admitted that "too often though, these programmes are pursued in isolation".[37] Almost a decade after the 2007 OECD-DAC *Handbook* made this admission, and despite growing enthusiasm for joined-up approaches to development and security assistance, SSR, SALW and DDR programmes are still characteristically advanced in a stand-alone manner, supported by their own dedicated resources, institutional machinery and cadre of technical experts. This has contributed to the disconnected patchwork of initiatives that comprises most modern peacebuilding and statebuilding projects – a stark contrast to the image of seamless and interconnected programming painted in many policy and strategy documents.

It is important to note the differing historical trajectories of the SSR, SALW and DDR agendas and how they have influenced the evolution of their interrelationships. The SALW and DDR projects, which first gained prominence in the late 1980s, predate the SSR model by more than a decade. SALW reduction and control programmes launched in countries like Cambodia, Colombia, El Salvador, Macedonia, Mali, Mozambique and South Africa in the mid-1990s garnered significant attention and firmly established the project in the modern peacebuilding toolkit. The rationale behind SALW reduction and control in FFCAS was straightforward, as the World Health Organization articulated in a 2003 report: the "availability of small arms and light weapons is an important factor in increasing the lethality of violent situations".[38] In other words, SALW in FFCAS situations act as "violence multipliers" whose "availability can generate a vicious circle of insecurity that, in turn, leads to greater demand for, and use of, small arms".[39] Of course, predatory and dysfunctional security institutions can exacerbate this vicious cycle and thereby deepen the security dilemma for communities in a way that drives demand for weapons.

In its early iterations SALW programming did not stray far from its core goal of removing surplus and illicit weapons from state and non-state hands; more ambitious and protracted imperatives of weapons regulation and community violence reduction were largely ancillary goals, which made the project more politically and operationally palatable than the transformative SSR model.[40] Indeed, as Bourne and Greene explain, despite the emergence of a preliminary SSR agenda by 2007–2008, the "very principle of supporting SSR was contested"[41] by parts of the UN Security Council, UN General Assembly and key bilateral powers such as Russia, China, India and Brazil. These states are "worried that national sovereignty might be unduly undermined by endorsing relatively intrusive engagements by UN peace-support missions to reform or shape internal security and governance institutions".[42] Such concerns of recipient states over potential transgressions of sovereignty were less pronounced for SALW programmes.

Although sharing a conceptual affinity, the best practices, systems and structures comprising the SALW agenda evolved independently of its SSR cousin, with SALW practitioners reluctant to attach themselves to an SSR model perceived as controversial in many quarters.[43] The more ambitious SSR agenda was enabled by the end of the Cold War and the space it opened up for new thinking on the security–development nexus.[44] While SSR was rapidly established as a core pillar of peacebuilding and statebuilding interventions in FFCAS alongside the more established SALW and DDR projects, its implementation has always faced more pronounced political hurdles that have limited its impacts.[45]

While innate synergies between the SSR and SALW projects are widely recognized by analysts and practitioners of both, the idea of overt integration of the two agendas has not achieved much traction. SALW analysts and practitioners are reticent to support the idea of subsuming the SALW project under the SSR agenda.[46] This is motivated by a concern that SALW programming could become a mere "tool" to achieve wider national security reform objectives, to the detriment of local community-based, human-security-driven SALW reduction and control activities.[47] Perhaps validating this concern, Bourne and Green explain how "international policy-makers and programmers responsible for promoting SSR have tended to focus on wider institutional reform objectives, regarding SALW control issues to be a side issue for SSR to be addressed later or by others".[48] Whether motivated by a parochial interest in protecting turf, a desire to preserve scarce resources or concerns over programmatic and political incompatibility, SSR and SALW policymakers and practitioners have not pressed to advance the integration of their agendas. The problem is that this failure to harmonize and integrate may have significantly reduced the efficacy of both projects in the field.

The SSR-SALW link in the SSR policy discourse

It is generally accepted that initiatives to mitigate the threat posed by the proliferation and misuse of SALW can facilitate SSR. The success of the SSR model is dependent on the presence of a number of specific conditions, one of which is a permissive security environment. The ready availability of SALW can lead to increased crime and violence, undermining human security and placing tremendous pressure on a transitioning security sector. In their 31-country study on "Socio-economic determinants of homicide and civil war", Collier and Hoeffler found that in the first five years following a civil war the homicide rate "is around 25% higher than normal".[49] For instance, El Salvador and Guatemala saw massive increases in violent crime in the years following their civil wars in the 1990s. They still have some of the highest homicide rates in the world.[50] It is not definitively clear how the availability of SALW factored into this elevated homicide rate, but it likely played a significant role. The proliferation of weapons can also disrupt political and peace processes by increasing the probability that political disputes will degenerate into armed conflict. Accordingly, efforts to address the problem of SALW proliferation are viewed in SSR policy literature as an important enabler of reform, particularly at the beginning of the process. As Powell notes, "large-scale disarmament of the civilian population is critical to create conditions under which a reformed police and military can fulfill their responsibilities to serve and protect the state and its population as well as to help contribute to community development and – ultimately – sustainable peace".[51] The UK Department for International Development (DFID) identifies two central pillars of SALW reduction and control programming that could be undertaken in close cooperation with SSR:

- Restoring effective mechanisms to maintain public security and regulate gun ownership.
- Increasing state capacity to monitor, check and prevent illegal arms transfers and to collect and destroy surplus weapons.[52]

While SSR processes benefit from SALW reduction and control measures to foster security conditions conducive for comprehensive reform, it is, in turn, the outcome and impact of those reforms that will determine the long-term efficacy of the SALW programme. Di Chiaro states that the "lack of a trained and effective police force and the subsequent absence of a secure environment have been identified as perhaps the greatest obstacle to effective weapons collection efforts" and has spurred "the continued demand for weapons".[53] Kreutz et al. concur with this point, explaining that "during an armed conflict, non-combatants are profoundly insecure and law enforcement might not function properly. In such circumstances, people will often obtain weapons for personal protection, even banding together to protect communities."[54] For instance, N'Diaye notes that in the Central African Republic "armed groups justify their existence and their right to use arms as a response to the repressive behaviour of the state security sector" – a common refrain of non-state armed groups in a variety of FFCAS.[55] From the same logic Chanaa argues that core elements of SSR such as "reforming the police, national guard, gendarmerie and customs authority" are indispensible for the goal of putting "a stop to the transfer of small arms".[56]

Bourne and Greene affirm that SSR and SALW programmes are deeply interconnected "because effective security and justice systems and agencies are essential for effective SALW governance and control".[57] The OECD-DAC's report, *Security System Reform: Policy and Good Practice*, emphasizes that:

> In an SSR context, the restoration of effective mechanisms to maintain public security and an appropriate regulation framework for small arms represents the best long-term response [to SALW proliferation], as can increased state capacity to monitor, check and prevent illegal arms transfers and collect and destroy surplus weapons.[58]

In other words, both demand- and supply-side approaches to SALW control can be advanced in parallel under the auspices of the SSR model.

The UN's Integrated DDR Standards[59] (IDDRS) succinctly states:

> SALW control measures are ... closely linked to SSR because they depend on the enforcement capacity of the police, the ability of border management bodies to restrict illicit flows of these weapons across borders as well as security sector oversight and accountability mechanisms to ensure appropriate control over national stocks.[60]

In this way the IDDRS sees SALW control processes as an important entry point for coordination between SSR and DDR: "SALW control measures should form part of joint assessments and be reflected in the design of DDR/SSR programmes."[61] Taking this idea of SALW as an entry point even further, the OECD-DAC *Handbook on Security System Reform* identifies the removal and control of SALW as a key launching pad for the entire SSR process, given that it presents a clear problem that SSR can be framed to address.[62] Therefore advancing SALW can play a vital role in justifying and legitimizing SSR.

In a 2004 SSR strategy paper the UK government highlighted the plethora of processes and tools within the scope of SSR that can be utilized to further SALW reduction and control objectives, including the promotion of comprehensive DDR programmes for former combatants; the enhancement of customs and border security; the strengthening of weapons stockpile management and the destruction of surplus weapons; the elaboration and rationalization of regulations and procedures regarding the use of weapons by statutory security forces; the development of centralized procurement systems; and the regulation of private security forces.[63] To this list can be added the process to develop and implement legislation and legal statutes to regulate the possession of weapons, including licensing regimes and weapons registries; the provision of specialized training to security forces to enhance their capacity to combat arms trafficking and oversee weapons collection operations; and awareness-raising activities to restore public confidence in the security forces and thereby encourage voluntary disarmament.[64] The European Union (EU), in its Programme for Preventing and Combating Illicit Trafficking in Conventional Arms, calls upon its member states to employ many of these tools when providing assistance to third countries, notably legal and administrative support, police and customs training, adoption of anti-corruption measures and promotion of regional, subregional and national cooperation among police forces, customs authorities and intelligence services.[65]

The most direct connection between SSR and SALW programming is the imperative to manage and/or reduce the SALW stocks of state security forces. The Small Arms Survey estimates that, taken together, state security forces – including the military, regular police, customs authorities, border police and other law enforcement agencies – control roughly one-quarter of the global arms stockpile. The problem lies in the fact that "inadequate firearm training of state agents, as well as insufficient safeguards on stocks, can lead to the illegitimate use of these weapons, their diversion to unauthorized groups or individuals, and the occurrence of deadly ammunition depot explosions".[66] Indeed, such occurrences are all too common in conflict-affected contexts. Weapons leakage "facilitated by weakness in physical security measures, accounting and record-keeping procedures" has fuelled insurgencies, supplied extremist groups and served as a major source of revenue for criminal organizations.[67] Accordingly, strengthening the capacity of the security sector to manage and oversee its arms holdings can shut off an important source of SALW proliferation and contain a major driver of violence.[68] Moreover, it can build the public confidence necessary to encourage voluntary community disarmament initiatives. After all, "in post-conflict contexts, few people trust the security institutions to keep collected weapons safe or dispose of them responsibly. They suspect instead – and with good reason – that they will be corruptly sold or lost, and later handed over to groups that contribute to their insecurity."[69] SSR can help solve the trust dilemma that so often undermines SALW reduction and control programmes.

As this section demonstrates, SSR policy literature lays out numerous practical linkages and overlaps between the SSR and SALW fields that can be exploited for their mutual benefit. These conceptual and technical ties have also been prominently presented and codified in key international agreements and protocols on SALW reduction and control, as the next section outlines.

The SSR–SALW link in SALW policy documents

Many of the international agreements and protocols developed to confront the problem of SALW proliferation feature clear provisions mandating the implementation of related and complementary reforms of the security sector. This section offers an overview of some of these key documents, with a distinct focus on the African continent, where the urgent need for SALW action has generated some of the most advanced thinking on the issue. The problem lies in the fact that this innovative thinking has not always translated into concrete action on the ground, particularly when it comes to the actualization of stronger SSR–SALW programmatic linkages.

A critical starting point for any analysis of international strategies and frameworks to address the SALW issue is the 2001 UN Programme of Action to Prevent, Combat and Eradicate the Illicit Trade in Small Arms and Light Weapons in All Its Aspects, which affirms that:

> States and international and regional organizations should seriously consider assisting interested states, upon request, in building capacities in

areas including the development of appropriate legislation and regulations, law enforcement, tracing and marking, stockpile management and security, destruction of small arms and light weapons and the collection and exchange of information.[70]

The programme of action recommends enhanced cooperation and information exchange "among competent officials, including customs, police, intelligence and arms control officials, at the national, regional and global levels".[71] It contains national, regional and global commitments to prevent, combat and eradicate the illicit trade in SALW, encompassing a wide array of issues including manufacturing, marking, tracing, stockpile management, international transfers, public awareness and DDR.

While the programme of action was a binding agreement, no mechanisms existed to enforce the compliance of signatories. Nonetheless, it provided the crucial foundation and framework for action on SALW globally, and was supplemented by other key UN conventions seeking to control SALW, such as the Protocol against the Illicit Manufacturing of and Trafficking in Firearms, Their Parts and Components and Ammunition, supplementing the UN Convention against Transnational Organized Crime and the Register of Conventional Arms.

National and regional-level accords on SALW have gone even further than the programme of action in outlining reforms within the security sector that are needed to ensure the viability of SALW reduction and control efforts. Five regional agreements in Africa – the Nairobi Declaration, the Economic Community of West African States (ECOWAS) Moratorium, the Bamako Declaration, the Southern African Development Community (SADC) Protocol and the AU Strategy on the Control of Illicit Proliferation, Circulation and Trafficking of Small Arms and Light Weapons – have been particularly explicit in making the causal link between effective SALW reduction and control programming and far-reaching SSR.

The 2000 Nairobi Declaration formalized a partnership among a wide array of actors, including governments, multilateral organizations and repre-sentatives of civil society, to address the problem of SALW proliferation in the Great Lakes region and the Horn of Africa. It was followed by the release of a "co-ordinated agenda for action" that set out clear guidelines and benchmarks for the signatory states to realize the declaration's overarching objectives. The agenda called on the state parties to the agreement to "develop or improve national training programmes to enhance the capacity of law enforcement agencies to fulfil their roles in the implementation of this agenda for action".[72]

It also recommended that the signatories "encourage regional co-operation for law enforcement and other relevant international agencies/bodies so as to combat cross-border crime, enhance human security, and foster understanding among border communities".[73] The East African Police Chiefs Cooperation Organization is identified in the agenda as a body whose extensive experience in dealing with cross-border illicit activities, including the trafficking of firearms, would enable it to advance regional collaboration and capacity building in relation to SALW. Legislative and legal reform is also identified as an integral facet of efforts to meet the declaration's objectives. The agenda's implementation plan outlined the need for a degree of legal uniformity in the East African region on SALW issues and prescribed the formation of minimum standards governing the manufacture, possession, import, export, transfer, transit, transport and control of SALW.[74] This process of creating and revising legislation and reforming and restructuring the judicial and legal apparatus falls squarely within the remit of the SSR agenda.

The Nairobi Declaration paved the way for the Nairobi Protocol for the Prevention, Control, and Reduction of Small Arms and Light Weapons in the Great Lakes Region and the Horn of Africa, adopted on 21 April 2004 in Nairobi, Kenya. The protocol, which entered into force on 5 May 2006, is a legally binding instrument that requires the implementation of a series of legislative measures by its signatories as well as efforts to enhance state capacity to manage and control weapons in the hands of state and non-state actors. The Regional Centre on Small Arms is responsible for supporting national focal points to implement the provisions of the declaration and protocol. It has implemented a wide array of projects, including arms marking exercises, arms destruction initiatives, stockpile management seminars, workshops for parliamentarians on outreach and public information, joint workshops with civil society actors, applied research into key SALW issues and the development of a training curriculum and manual for law enforcement bodies.[75] Many of these projects directly overlap with SSR programmes in individual countries.

The 1998 ECOWAS Moratorium on the Importation, Exportation and Manufacture of Small Arms and Light Weapons in West Africa contained more robust mechanisms to ensure integrated SSR–SALW programming. The moratorium emanated from efforts to find a durable peace for civil-war-stricken Malawi. Cognizant that regional arms flows were a significant driver of the conflict, Malawian President Alpha Konare proposed a regional freeze on the import, export and manufacturing of light weapons in West Africa. The three-year renewable agreement was signed by the ECOWAS member states on 31 October

1998 and came into force on 1 November 1998. It was renewed twice, the last time being in October 2004.

The moratorium comprised three main instruments: the moratorium declaration; a code of conduct that outlined a series of objectives for the signatories and guidelines for the development of policy; and the Plan of Action for Coordination and Assistance on Security and Development (PCASED), a project run by the UN Development Programme (UNDP) intended to oversee SSR that would facilitate SALW reduction and control efforts.[76] Improving the overall capacity and capability of state security forces and the development of a comprehensive regulatory regime to confront SALW were the underlying objectives of the PCASED. However, since the purpose of the moratorium was to prevent imports of arms into a country, much of the focus of the PCASED was on strengthening border and customs police infrastructure and practices. An example of an initiative supported by the PCASED is the development of a training curriculum on modern methods of arms control, which evolved into a manual for the security forces.[77] The manual, produced with support from ECOWAS and the UN Regional Centre for Peace and Disarmament in Africa, based in Lomé, Togo, had three objectives:[78]

- Sensitizing the security forces concerning the threat posed by SALW proliferation.
- Expanding the technical capacity of the security forces to implement weapons collection programmes, facilitate DDR of ex-combatants, manage weapons stockpiles and enforce complex regulatory frameworks.
- Enhancing the overall quality and effectiveness of law enforcement agencies to confront related threats such as drug and human trafficking and reduce overall levels of insecurity that stimulate the demand for arms.

While the PCASED had a robust mandate to advance reforms in the security sector that could jump-start SALW reduction and control efforts, its impact was marginal. Vines attributes this to the weak capacity of ECOWAS. According to Vines, donors and UN agencies need to improve coordination among themselves and with ECOWAS concerning capacity building and invest more in "strategic areas of police capacity-building, security sector reform, and the disarmament and demobilization of ex-combatants".[79] This is hardly a novel idea, as shortfalls in capacity, resources and political will have perennially been the principal obstacles to the operationalization of SSR and SALW programmes.

According to the Small Arms Survey, "poor monitoring and weak government structures, and the fact that the moratorium was not legally binding, undermined its effectiveness", leading to its replacement by the ECOWAS Convention on Small Arms and Light Weapons, Their Ammunition and Other Related Materials in 2006.[80] The convention prohibits all international transfers of SALW within the region unless the ECOWAS Secretariat gives an exemption. Among other provisions, it places strict controls on SALW manufacturing; establishes measures to encourage information sharing on SALW among member states; and presents guidelines on civilian possession, stockpile security and marking, tracing and brokering of SALW.[81]

Another important SALW milestone came in 2000 when the Organization of African Unity, drawing on the Nairobi Declaration and ECOWAS Moratorium, set out a common position on SALW in time for the 2001 UN Conference on the Illicit Trade in Small Arms and Light Weapons in All Its Aspects. Engineered at a ministerial meeting in Bamako, Mali, the agreement came to be known as the Bamako Declaration. The declaration contained clear language on the importance of SSR to SALW reduction and control efforts, recommending that the state parties "enhance the capacity of national law enforcement and security agencies and officials to deal with all aspects of the arms problem, including appropriate training on investigative procedures, border control and specialized actions, and upgrading of equipment and resources".[82] It also called for legislative and legal measures "to establish as a criminal offence under national law, the illicit manufacturing of, trafficking in, and illegal possession and use of small arms and light weapons, ammunition and other related materials".[83] The declaration reflected growing emphasis on the security sector as the locus for effective SALW control efforts, but failed to elucidate adequately how this relationship should be operationalized.

The Protocol on the Control of Firearms, Ammunition, and Other Related Materials in the Southern African Development Community Region was adopted by the SADC in August 2001. Like the Nairobi Declaration, ECOWAS Moratorium and Bamako Declaration, the SADC Protocol acknowledged the inextricable relationship between efforts to limit SALW availability and the development of an efficient, effective and democratically governed security sector that can fulfil its place as the security guarantor of the population. The protocol committed state parties to "undertake to improve the capacity of police, customs, border guards, the military, the judiciary and other relevant agencies".[84] More specifically, it obligated member states to coordinate national training programmes for the different security sector actors involved in SALW control; to create and improve communications and information management systems to monitor and track regional arms flows; and to enhance interagency and regional cooperation among relevant agencies.[85] Consistent with the prominent role accorded to law enforcement and the enactment of SSR in the protocol, the Southern African Regional Police Chiefs Cooperation Organization (SARPCCO) was accorded a lead role in its implementation. SARPCCO was tasked with overseeing training for regional law enforcement agencies on technical and procedural issues related to SALW control, and establishing mechanisms to enhance regional coordination and information sharing. The role of SARPCCO was viewed by many observers as extremely constructive and beneficial for the process and a potential model for other regions.[86]

On 30 April 2011 the 11 member states of the UN Standing Advisory Committee on Security Questions in Central Africa unanimously endorsed the Central African Convention for the Control of Small Arms and Light Weapons, Their Ammunition, Parts and Components that Can Be Used for Their Manufacture, Repair or Assembly, also known as the Kinshasa Convention (given the location of its signing). Like the previous conventions produced by ECOWAS and the SADC, the purpose of the agreement was manifold: to "prevent, combat and eradicate" the illicit trade and trafficking of SALW in Central Africa; to establish border controls over the "manufacture, trade, movement, transfer, possession and use" of SALW; to reduce violence and suffering brought about by SALW; and to foster regional dialogue and cooperation.[87] The agreement called on its signatories to create laws, regulations and a licensing system that would prohibit the possession and use of firearms by unlicensed civilians, along with appropriate penalties for transgressors.[88] The agreement mandated improvements in stockpile management and the expansion of border controls "to put an end in Central Africa to the illicit traffic" in SALW.[89] The section on border control went as far as to recommend strengthening multilateral cooperation at borders, including the organization of "joint and mixed trans-border operations and patrols".[90] The agreement called for the establishment of a "system of judicial cooperation" involving the sharing and "exchange of information through the customs, police, water and forest services, the gendarmerie, the border guards or any other competent State body".[91] Anti-corruption measures across the state and security sectors also formed a major part of the agreement.[92] The convention is one of the most thorough established to date, recognizing the conceptual and policy advances made in the SALW reduction and control field as well as the wide acceptance of the dangers that SALW pose to peace, security and political stability in Africa. It also draws very explicit and in many cases innovative linkages between

SSR and SALW action. While implementation has not met the high expectations that greeted the signing of the convention, its adoption alongside that of the AU strategy of the same year represents a watershed in the field.

In 2011 the AU adopted the AU Strategy on the Control of Illicit Proliferation, Circulation and Trafficking of Small Arms and Light Weapons. The strategy set out to "address comprehensively the problem of the illicit proliferation, circulation and trafficking of small arms and light weapons through mainstreaming SALW control as a cross-cutting and multidimensional issue in achieving peace, security, development, and stability in the Continent".[93] It empowered the AU Regions Steering Committee on Small Arms, a group comprising ten AU regional economic communities (RECs) and two observers in 2008,[94] to oversee the implementation of the SALW strategy by national governments, the RECs and the AU Commission. The committee was also mandated to engage civil society actors and regional police organizations to advance the goals of the new AU strategy.[95] The strategy explicitly recognized the holistic nature of the SALW issue, requiring interventions in the security and development spheres, including SSR.

A watershed for the SALW issue globally came on 2 April 2013 when the UN General Assembly adopted the Arms Trade Treaty, complementing previous regional and global instruments.[96] The landmark agreement signed by 130 states represented the most comprehensive global framework for conventional arms control ever established. Under Article 16 on international assistance, the treaty states that parties to the agreement may seek assistance – whether legislative, institutional capacity building, technical, material or financial – from "the United Nations, international, regional, subregional or national organizations, non-governmental organizations, or on a bilateral basis". The assistance could include "Stockpile management, disarmament, demobilization and reintegration programmes, model legislation, and effective practices for implementation."[97] The treaty clearly recognizes the indispensible nature of reforms in the security sector for the successful application SALW reduction and control.

The preceding analysis of recent SALW reduction and control agreements and protocols demonstrates the extent to which SSR has come to occupy a central place in SALW thinking and policy. SSR, by expanding the capacity of the state to regulate gun possession, secure state stockpiles, curb illegal trafficking, entrench the rule of law and provide the populace with a security guarantee, endeavours simultaneously to curtail the supply of arms and to reduce public demand for their acquisition. It creates the institutional conditions in which SALW reduction programmes launched in FFCAS can evolve into long-term weapons control regimes. However, while policymakers have recognized the intrinsic links between SSR and SALW programming, their relationship at the operational level remains underdeveloped. As the Centre for Humanitarian Dialogue noted in a 2007 report, "to date, justice and security sector reform efforts have generally not been informed by current thinking on best practices on small arms controls – and vice versa".[98] The same could be said today. The innumerable provisions on security sector capacity building and reforms encapsulated in the principal conventions on SALW have rarely been translated effectively into practice. In the field, the implementation of SSR and SALW reduction and control programmes continues to be advanced on parallel but separate tracks – only loosely connected under the peacebuilding banner – rather than as a single integrated framework of action as stipulated by both SSR orthodoxy and key SALW agreements and protocols.

Practical areas of SSR–SALW convergence

There are numerous practical areas of convergence between SSR and SALW programming. SALW reduction and control programmes address both the tools of violence and the associated political, economic and social dynamics that drive and shape their possession, proliferation and (mis)use. The focus of SSR programming as it pertains to SALW extends well beyond arming state security actors – once the overriding purpose of Western security assistance – to prioritizing the development of state capacity to manage and regulate weapons stocks. A major goal of SSR programmes is to establish the software (legal norms, legislative mechanisms, accountability structures and human capacity) to exercise effective control over the hardware of the security system – the instruments of violence and the security forces that wield them. Accordingly, the reform and transformation of dysfunctional security sectors in transition states can be important enablers for efforts to reduce and control SALW.

Few would disagree that the uncontrolled circulation of unlicensed weapons, ammunition and explosive materials can be a source of insecurity in any environment, particularly areas recovering from armed conflict or state failure. As a 2013 UN report states, "if illicit weapons continue to be easily accessible to armed groups and civilians in post-conflict situations, the risk of relapse into conflict will remain high and the prospects of building a sustainable peace will diminish even if efforts are made to dismantle armed groups and movements".[99] Beyond merely the resumption of political violence, the widespread availability of arms can also drive criminality. With this in mind, the OECD-DAC *Handbook on*

Security System Reform recognized that "programmes to control the spread of small arms can play an important role in peacebuilding and in reducing insecurity and armed violence, in both post-conflict countries and other developing transitional societies".[100] The indispensible role SSR can play in facilitating the SALW reduction and control agenda is laid out well by the UN:

> [S]ince small arms are typically traced through national police and other law enforcement agencies, United Nations police components in the field, regional and subregional police organizations and INTERPOL subregional bureaus, in particular, could play an important role in building the capacity of national authorities in the marking and tracing of weapons, record-keeping and stockpile security ... [101]

It is important to note that of the 875 million firearms in the world in 2012, as estimated by the Small Arms Survey, 225 million were in the hands of state security forces and 650 million in private possession.[102] The security sector plays a vital role in controlling both categories, by creating sound stockpile management and control procedures for state security stocks, and managing regulatory regimes and reduction programmes for the weapons circulating in the public domain.

SALW programmes engage a variety of different actors in the security sector – from police and customs services to border control and judicial officials – "and focus on strengthening governance and capacity".[103] Despite these multiple areas of convergence, "links to SSR programmes are rarely made in practice".[104] Indeed, Bourne and Greene explain that although "in principle, strong synergies appear to be possible between supporting SSR and enhanced SALW governance and control", examples of how SSR programmes have influenced SALW reduction and control programming are "hard to discern".[105]

SSR and SALW programmes have short-, medium- and long-term dimensions, playing different roles in the lifespan of a security transition. One of the first tasks earmarked for implementation in the aftermath of a conflict is DDR, seen as a crucial to stabilize and secure the post-war environment and carve out space for the war-to-peace transition. DDR programmes may address the problem of weapons in the possession of wartime combatants, but they tend to have a minimal effect on overarching patterns of weapons possession and proliferation. Indeed, the disarmament pillar of the DDR triad is characteristically treated as symbolic, rather than a systematic effort to address conflict-driven weapons diffusion and possession.[106] To address wider issues of illicit weapons flows in the aftermath of conflict, longer-term SALW reduction and control initiatives are needed. While DDR plays a critical short-term stabilization role, SALW programming can consolidate peace and improve human security over the middle to long terms.

While SSR is typically understood to be a long-term, even generational, project, it also plays an important role in the early stages of a security transition. Whether referred to as security sector stabilization[107] or interim stabilization measures,[108] early SSR activity in FFCAS plays a crucial role in addressing security vacuums and building public confidence in the state. Re-establishing the legitimacy of the security sector in the aftermath of conflict or state collapse as quickly as possible is indispensible because "people will be unwilling to surrender their weapons while they are still in danger from armed groups and in the absence of effective provision of security".[109] Indeed, "visible progress on police reform is often vital to increase the public's perceptions of security as a precursor to weapons collection programmes".[110] It is also important to note that with resources typically in short supply in FFCAS, disarmament programmes may provide an important boost for SSR processes, given that "the collection of arms through the disarmament component of the DDR programme may in certain cases provide an important source of weapons for reformed security forces".[111]

There are several practical areas of convergence between SSR and SALW activity. This section concentrates on five: stockpile management, weapons procurement, border control, legal instruments for weapons control and DDR.

Stockpile management

A clear contribution of SSR to the broader goals of SALW reduction and control in FFCAS is the strengthening of stockpile management capacity in state security institutions.[112] UN Resolution 2117 recognizes the "value of effective physical security and management of stockpiles of small arms, light weapons and ammunition as an important means to prevent the illicit transfer, destabilizing accumulation and misuse of small arms and light weapons".[113] An August 2013 report of the UN Secretary-General on small arms affirmed that "stockpile management and control has emerged as one of the greatest challenges relating to small arms".[114] As Bromley et al. state, "the effective management of arms stockpiles, the destruction of surplus arms and the marking of arms on import have all been prescribed as means to combat the illicit arms trade".[115] Weapons leaked from state security institutions have often fuelled conflict and criminality in FFCAS. The UN Secretary-General's 2013 report summarized the ramifications of stockpile diversion well:

> [P]oorly managed government stockpiles remain prominent sources of illegal small arms circulating both within a country and across borders. Explosives or detonating cords can be stolen and used in the manufacture of improvised explosive devices, potentially contributing to terrorist activities. In the context of peacekeeping operations, the diversion of arms and ammunition from stockpiles of troop-contributing countries or from collected weapons creates additional force protection issues for peacekeepers, making an already challenging job more difficult. Poorly managed ammunition stockpiles pose an additional risk of explosion at great cost to human life, livelihoods and the environment.[116]

As the OECD-DAC *Handbook on Security System Reform* states, "a large percentage of weapons in the illicit market in many countries were stolen or sold from police and military stockpiles".[117] The IDDRS also cites the danger of weapons "leakage" due to "inadequately managed and controlled storage facilities" as a major driver of weapons proliferation and a public security threat.[118] Illustrating this problem, N'Diaye details how in the Central African Republic poorly paid members of the armed forces routinely "sold weapons to anyone who could pay for them", contributing "to the widespread availability of SALW among the populace".[119] In South Sudan leaked weapons from "stockpiles in neighbouring countries" swelled "community-based arsenals" and acted as a major driver of conflict.[120] Addressing this source of illicit SALW supply requires the strengthening of state capacity to manage weapons and ammunition stocks: "Conducting inventories of weapons stockpiles, ensuring they are secure, and destroying surplus stocks are important linkages between SSR and small arms control."[121]

Several important initiatives have been launched under the auspices of the UN to build stockpile management capacity in FFCAS. The UN has developed international technical guidelines for ammunition management as well as the International Small Arms Control Standards[122] guiding "weapons collection and destruction, stockpile management, marking, record-keeping and tracing".[123] For instance, the Accra-based Kofi Annan International Peacekeeping Training Centre provides training to government officials from ECOWAS countries on stockpile management, marking, record keeping, tracing and border security management.[124] As of 2013, the UN Regional Centre for Peace, Disarmament and Development in Latin America and the Caribbean had carried out more than 70 assistance activities in the area of stockpile management, including "training more than 430 national security sector officers on small arms control issues".[125]

Despite this UN activity, most stockpile management capacity-building programmes are bilateral, carried out by state militaries or subcontracted to private security companies (PSCs). UN Resolution 2117 welcomed the "efforts made by Member States, regional and sub-regional organizations in addressing the illicit transfer, destabilizing accumulation and misuse of small arms and light weapons", but also encouraged:

> [T]he establishment or strengthening, where appropriate, of sub-regional and regional cooperation, coordination and information-sharing mechanisms, in particular, trans-border customs cooperation and networks for information-sharing, with a view to preventing, combating, and eradicating illicit transfer, destabilizing accumulation and misuse of small arms and light weapons.[126]

The resolution further established that "peacekeeping operations and relevant [Security] Council mandated entities may assist" in addressing:

> [T]he illicit trafficking of small arms and light weapons, including inter alia through weapons collection, disarmament, demobilization, and reintegration programmes, enhancing physical security and stockpile management practices, record keeping and tracing capacities development of national export and import control systems, enhancement of border security, and strengthening judicial institutions and law enforcement capacity.[127]

The UN is increasingly mainstreaming SALW stockpile management assistance in its peacebuilding and statebuilding agendas.

It is noteworthy that a specialized UN instrument, the UN SaferGuard Programme, has been established to assist states in ammunition stockpile management. The programme includes "a quick-response mechanism that allows for the rapid deployment of ammunition experts in response to requests from Member States for assistance in securing ammunition stockpiles".[128] Ammunition is often an afterthought of SALW programmes, but tends to be more widely disbursed and versatile in its destructive uses than conventional small arms (e.g. for the creation of improvised explosive devices), and thus can pose a more serious public safety risk. The SaferGuard Programme represents the type of standing capacity that the UN would like to see established at the regional level for broader SALW stockpile management.

Weapons procurement

States recovering from conflict face distinct and often acute security challenges. Although FFCAS tend to be awash with weaponry – much of it outside state control – state weapons holdings may be outdated or insufficient to address the country's security needs. Under such circumstances, states in transition may need to procure SALW from external sources, necessitating the establishment of procurement policies and systems. The dangers of advancing procurement processes in the absence of robust regulatory procedures and systems are manifest, as outlined by Bromley et al.:

> Post-shipment diversion refers to situations in which arms are transferred to an end-user (e.g. rebel, terrorist etc.) other than the intended end-user, without the express authorization of the exporting state's relevant authorities. Diversion can occur in state-to-state transfers and in transfers involving commercial suppliers. Post-shipment diversion is a worrying and common feature of arms and ammunition transfers to national security forces in fragile states, as weapons have subsequently been found in the hands of actors that are seeking to undermine stabilization efforts and intensify or resume armed conflict in the fragile state or its neighbourhood.[129]

The diversion of arms shipments in FFCAS can stoke conflict, create new fault-lines of tension and facilitate a rise in criminal violence. Some international instruments have been established to help combat SALW diversion, such as notification systems for arms transfers by suppliers, but much of the oversight onus is invariably placed on recipients. The problem this poses is, as Bromley et al. note, that "training on good procedures in the procurement of arms and ammunition are often absent from SSR activities".[130] For instance, while the European Council's SSR concept document calls for attention to be paid to building procurement capacity in line security ministries and agencies of FFCAS, there are no concrete examples where such activity has formed a significant part of an EU-sponsored SSR programme.[131] One of the problems in the SSR community is that there has been minimal guidance on how to support the development of procurement capacity. The OECD-DAC *Handbook on Security System Reform* discusses issues of public finance management and improving defence budgeting, but does "not detail how to manage specific acquisitions and minimize the associated risks" of diversion and mismanagement.[132] Given that transfers of leaked weapons and the general undermining of procurement systems can be a source of instability and a driver of corruption within the security sector and beyond, SALW procurement should be a critical target for SSR assistance.[133]

Border control

A central point of intersection between SSR and SALW activity is border control. Strengthening border security and customs infrastructure in FFCAS is critical to arresting cross-border weapons flows. A 2010 Saferworld report on strengthening border management under the UN programme of action emphasized "the importance of embedding initiatives to enhance border controls within comprehensive national and regional SALW control strategies".[134] Karp also highlights how effectively controlled borders establish "preferred circumstances for effective civilian collection" of SALW.[135]

Several factors have hindered efforts to combat cross-border SALW flows and trafficking in borderlands, including the vast and remote nature of many state boundaries; inadequate cooperation and coordination among neighbouring states; competing priorities for governments; lack of a comprehensive SALW plan; poorly paid and trained border and customs services; outdated border surveillance and management equipment; corruption and clientelism; and underdeveloped or poorly designed border control policies.[136] In various agreements, reports and resolutions the UN has called for the promotion of links between SALW programmes and SSR to overcome these challenges. As the Saferworld report explains:

> [SSR] in this context includes reforms to improve the effectiveness and accountability of border control agencies such as border guards, coast-guards, airport and air traffic control authorities, maritime and port authorities, immigration agencies and customs.[137]

The report goes on to recommend that in addition to providing direct assistance to develop border management capacity, the UN should recognize the need, under the auspices of SSR, "to address the security, law-enforcement justice and dispute-resolution needs and concerns of citizens and communities, particularly of those communities whose co-operation is important for effective border management (e.g. borderland communities, business and trading communities, air, sea and land transportation sector workers)".[138] Cross-border communities play just as important a role in border control as the physical infrastructure and the security personnel assigned to enforce it.

Integration has become one of the buzzwords of border management reforms in the context of SSR and SALW. According to a 2012 UN report, a state's ability to "deter, detect and intercept illicit movements of small arms and light weapons" is predicated on the ability of "law enforcement agencies – in particular customs, immigration and border police – [to] coordinate and cooperate with one another, both within their own countries and with their counterparts on the opposite side of the border".[139] This entails integrating military, law enforcement and intelligence agencies and customs bodies within and among states – a daunting task in any context, and particularly in low-income countries recovering from internecine conflict or state failure. However, it reflects the intrinsic holistic vision of the SSR model, which views the various pillars of the security and justice systems as deeply intertwined and mutually reinforcing. This call for cross-border integration of border management capacities to combat illicit weapons flows should also encompass SALW reduction and control initiatives. Despite some ambitious agreements and protocols calling for regional cooperation on SALW reduction and control, as described earlier, few effective regional implementation frameworks have been established.

Legal instruments for weapons control and oversight
SALW programmes overlap with judicial and legal reform processes in FFCAS. To establish an effective weapons management and control regime, specialized laws are needed to govern weapons ownership and possession. The 2008 UNDP *How-to Guide on Small Arms and Light Weapons Legislation* explained:

> Comprehensive and harmonized laws – within a nation and amongst neighbouring nations – provide a framework for regulating weapons manufacture, possession, storage, transfer and use, setting the parameters for permissible behaviour and practice, and providing measures for enforcement.[140]

Specialized legal statutes may also be needed to regulate PSCs and their access to weapons. As the OECD-DAC *Handbook on Security System Reform* states, "introducing regulation and oversight of the use of firearms by PSCs can be an important component of national small arms control strategies and action plans".[141] The drafting of laws regulating SALW also has to be matched by the expansion of law enforcement and judicial capacity to uphold them, and the regulatory machinery to monitor weapons ownership. Donor assistance will invariably be required to develop weapons registration and tracing systems mandated by weapons laws. Legal frameworks alone cannot arrest SALW proliferation:

> [I]t needs to be complemented ... by measures as diverse as police reform, employment schemes, reconciliation efforts, urban planning and youth programmes which can influence the demand for weapons and individual's behaviour and compliance with laws.[142]

Police and other internal security bodies require the capacity to enforce legislation as well as any instruments of arms control they establish, like licensing schemes or weapons registries. These are technically demanding processes that are also prone to mismanagement and corruption. Well-trained, resourced and governed security structures – the principal product of successful SSR – are required to manage such complex systems.

The disarmament, demobilization and reintegration of former combatants
The most obvious area of convergence for SSR and SALW programming in FFCAS is DDR, referred to by former UN Secretary-General Kofi Annan in 2006 as "a prerequisite for post-conflict stability and recovery".[143] DDR programmes have become a staple of UN peacebuilding missions over the past decade, widely seen as one of the first steps of democratic transitions in FFCAS. In fact, "since 1999, DDR has been a part of the mandate of all peacekeeping operations and a large number of special political missions in the field".[144] In 2009 alone the roughly $1.6 billion dedicated to DDR programmes was "25 times the total amount allocated in any one year for destruction of state small arms, light weapons, and ammunition surpluses".[145] According to Muggah and O'Donnell, "no fewer than 60 separate DDR initiatives were fielded around the world since the late 1980s",[146] covering a broad swathe of the globe. The level of DDR activity has grown dramatically over the past two decades: in 2013 "estimated mandated caseloads for on-going DDR operations in peacekeeping contexts alone were over 400,000".[147]

As the UN explains prominently on its website, by "removing weapons from the hands of combatants, taking the combatants out of military structures, and integrating combatants socially and economically into society", DDR programmes aim to "create an enabling environment for political and peace processes by dealing with security problems that arise when ex-combatants are trying to adjust to normal life, during the vital transition period from conflict to peace and development".[148] DDR should help to foster enabling security conditions for the reform of security institutions and create the structural framework and momentum for wider SALW reduction and control initiatives. In other words, it should provide space for the development of productive linkages between SSR and SALW programmes during their formative stages.

The DDR concept has evolved considerably since its inception in the 1990s. According to some analysts and observers like Muggah and O'Donnell, it is now in its third phase of development. DDR moved from a first wave that adopted a fairly technical and linear approach fixated on demobilizing warring parties after a peace agreement to a second-generation model focused more broadly on shaping conditions for sustainable peace and development after a political settlement, and then to the current "next-generation DDR" model that targets a variety of non-state armed actors outside conventional political settlements and is more attuned to issues of community violence reduction.[149] DDR orthodoxy has evolved and adjusted to changing global conflict dynamics, becoming more ambitious and more politically attuned over time.

In theory DDR provides an ideal entry point for SSR–SALW cooperation and integration, but in the first two waves of DDR programmes in the field often failed to cement enduring bonds with SSR and SALW projects. Bourne and Greene recognize that "local institution-building relating to DDR has typically been custom-made, with little attention to longer term local institution-building for either SALW control or SSR. Separately designed and managed programmes under each issue area have tended to resist more than minimal coordination."[150] One explanation for this lack of attention to cross-programme coordination is that DDR projects are transitory in nature, tending to last for periods of two to five years in the early stages of a transition, thereby providing limited time and space to form durable programmatic links.[151] Rather than being viewed as a foundation for wider multidisciplinary initiatives, DDR projects have tended to be treated as discrete stand-alone projects.

Current trends in DDR seem to favour greater integration with wider peacebuilding and statebuilding processes, including SSR and SALW programming, as part of a more holistic strategy to counter violent extremism and advance community violence reduction.[152] Such a trend can help create conditions for a more concerted push towards SSR–SALW integration, as DDR remains the most visible manifestation of the SSR–SALW nexus.

Disincentives for SSR–SALW integration

As the five areas of convergence demonstrate, the SSR and SALW fields intersect on a variety of pivotal issues where action or inaction can produce stabilizing or destabilizing effects. By highlighting the experience in a diverse array of case studies where SSR and SALW programmes have coexisted, the next section shows the impacts and implications of both successful and failed efforts to advance joined-up programming. However, before delving into the case studies it is important to touch on some of the disincentives for integration that may exist at both policy and implementation levels.

There are numerous disincentives for the integration of SSR and SALW projects, many of which have already been alluded to in this paper. First, the politically contentious nature of SSR efforts can make SALW projects reticent to support integration, fearing that the typical political volatility affecting SSR activities could spill over to SALW programming.[153]

Second, depending on the context, SSR and SALW programmes can operate with different timeframes, which has a profound effect on how they plan and relate to other pillars of wider peacebuilding and statebuilding projects.[154] SALW practitioners are often focused on the immediate challenges of SALW reduction and control in volatile and insecure environments, limiting the scope for consideration of the long-term implications of their activities for the security sector. Long-term outlooks are often viewed as a luxury for SALW practitioners in volatile implementation settings, limiting the incentives to seek coordination with SSR.

Third, the fact that the two fields have evolved as independent, with their own norms, principles, best practices, cadres of experts and communities of practice, has inhibited integration. There is a built-in bias towards maintaining their positions as discrete professional fields rather than as subpillars of a more ambitious project.

Fourth, from an institutional perspective the development of independent institutional resources and capacities at the state, intergovernmental and civil society levels to advance the two projects has made systemic coordination difficult. With so many specialist organizations focused on their own issue areas, there are significant costs for coordination. In the UN system several coordination mechanisms have been established to facilitate joint action among the variety of specialized agencies in the peacebuilding field, with the Inter-Agency Security Sector Reform Task Force being one example. The task force involves 14 UN bodies with a stake in SSR, including the UN Department for Disarmament Affairs (UNDDA), but this has not resulted in substantial improvements in SSR–SALW coordination on the ground.[155] The specialization of the SSR and DDR fields, while understandable considering the diverse and specialized technical demands of both, has perhaps obscured macro-strategic perspectives that favour integration.

It is also worth noting that there are significant start-up costs and resource demands involved in facilitating integration and enhanced collaboration between SSR and SALW actors and agencies, and many stakeholders are reluctant to incur these. Fostering horizontal, multidisciplinary collaboration in fields arranged more as vertical silos requires significant investments of human and institutional capacity. Overall, there are numerous factors that have militated against the integration of the SSR and SALW agendas. These obstacles are not insurmountable, but overcoming them will require concerted attention and action from all the key stakeholders in the two areas.

The SSR-SALW Link on the Ground

SSR and SALW reduction and control programmes have coexisted in a plethora of FFCAS cases over the past two decades. This paper argues that the manner in which the relationship between these two projects is framed, managed and leveraged affects their individual ground-level impacts. The case studies discussed here all satisfy the basic criteria of having well-developed SSR and SALW programmes which operated either concurrently or consecutively, as well as a significant international donor presence and meaningful external assistance in either SSR or SALW programming. Of course, there are many countries fitting these criteria, not all of which could be included in this paper. Among many possible choices, six case studies were selected to present a geographically diverse picture and illustrate a wide array of contextual circumstances. Geographically, the cases are located in Europe (Albania), Africa (Malawi and the DRC), Central Asia (Afghanistan), the Americas (El Salvador) and Southeast Asia (Cambodia). The cases cover a fragile state (Albania), a low-income developing state (Malawi), post-conflict environments (Cambodia and El Salvador) and conflict-affected and failed states (Afghanistan and the DRC). At a programmatic level, the cases differ in terms of the level of conflict present; the number and type of donors involved; the degree to which SSR–SALW linkages formed, and whether planned or opportunistic; the level of local ownership and leadership in SSR and SALW programming; and the type and quality of SSR and SALW impacts. The analysis of a diverse spectrum of case-study countries was intended to give a comprehensive picture of the experience of SSR–SALW integration.

While it is important to note that some of the examined cases, notably El Salvador and Albania, feature political and security transitions that predated the emergence of a coherent SSR model – as defined by key reference texts like the OECD-DAC *Handbook on Security System Reform* – they nonetheless involved extensive SSR-related activity, even if not categorized explicitly as such. A trend that can be detected across the cases is that the stronger the connective tissue between SSR and SALW programmes, the more effective and sustainable they have proven to be. Contextual conditions will invariably determine the viability of SSR and SALW programmes as well as the degree to which durable linkages between them can be formed, but the case-study analysis does seem to reveal marked utility in integrating SSR and SALW reduction and control programmes in all types of FFCAS.

The quality of SSR–SALW integration in FFCAS can be measured by a number of criteria, including the degree to which programming has been jointly planned, assessed and evaluated; the level of resource sharing and joint institutional and human capacity; and the coherence of their messaging and political approach. However, the best test of the overarching utility of integration is its impact on the effectiveness of the two fields in achieving their core goals. Four general questions informed the case-study analysis in assessing the extent of success or failure of SSR–SALW integration.

- Did SALW programming provide an entry point for SSR?
- Did SSR programming help to establish the necessary level of public trust and confidence in the security sector to facilitate community engagement in SALW activities?
- Did SALW programming help to shape a permissive security environment for SSR?
- Did SSR programmes forge the institutional structures and capacity needed to advance and consolidate long-term SALW control objectives?

Each case study features some background on the contextual conditions that faced SSR and SALW programming, and details the specific SSR and SALW initiatives undertaken. The scope, character and achievements (extent of success or failure) of the relationships between SSR and SALW activities are assessed, with the intent of identifying important insights and lessons. The cases are grouped into three categories according to an assessment of the outcomes and impacts of their SALW and SSR programming: successful, partially successful and failed.

Successful case

Malawi

Following independence in 1964, Malawi was ruled as a one-party state by the Malawi Congress Party (MCP) and its leader, Dr Kamuzu Banda. It was effectively a dictatorship for over 30 years until Banda – under pressure from strikes, demonstrations and riots – agreed to legalize opposition parties and hold elections. His successor, President Bakili Muluzi, inherited a dysfunctional security sector that was widely feared and mistrusted. The disarmament of the disbanded Malawi Young Pioneers, a political militia used by the MCP as an agent of repression, was "chaotic and incomplete", leaving many weapons unaccounted for.[156] Further complicating the SALW control situation, the security forces exercised very little control over Malawi's expansive and remote border areas.[157] Instability in neighbouring Mozambique and conflicts in the Great Lakes region drove the proliferation of SALW in Malawi. Since the mid-1990s the country has witnessed an upsurge in armed violence and crime, though overall rates are still low compared to other countries in sub-Saharan Africa. Nevertheless, the quantity of SALW in the possession of both criminal groups and the civilian population remains an area of concern.[158]

International donor support to Malawi's democratic transition has tended to draw strong linkages between civilian-focused SALW programming and SSR. As one report noted, "the Malawi model addresses the linkages between tackling small arms proliferation and reforming the security sector".[159] Community policing, which has been a centrepiece of the SSR agenda in Malawi since 1995 and enthusiastically endorsed by Malawi's government, has been an important vehicle for SSR–SALW integration. It forms "the grounding philosophy" of Malawi's policing, as the government's Malawi Police Service Strategic Development Plan 2011–2016 put it.[160] Inclusivity has also been a driving principle of SSR and SALW programme implementation, with civil society and community groups working hand in hand with the Malawi Police Service (MPS). From the outset of Malawi's security and political transition, an explicit link was made between the capacity of the police to provide security in a rights-respecting manner and the public demand for SALW.

SSR and SALW programming

One of the central SSR challenges in Malawi was the poor relationship between the police and the communities they serve.[161] Public suspicion and mistrust of the police jeopardized voluntary participation in SALW control programming.[162] Another major challenge was that the MPS was significantly underresourced compared to other police services in the region, and lacked training and specialist capacity in core areas related to SALW control such as stockpile management, ballistics and forensics. These capacity shortfalls encumbered the MPS in its efforts to combat SALW proliferation.[163] Even a decade after Malawi's adoption of multiparty democracy in 1993, the MPS remained "painfully aware of its incapacity to prevent small arms proliferation in the country".[164]

The Malawi Police Organisation Development Project (MALPOD) was a UK-funded programme to develop the organizational capacity of the MPS. Based on a community policing model, the project oversaw the creation of the Community Policing Services Branch of the MPS and the training of community police officers stationed at regional and district levels. One of the innovative components of the project was its formation of community policing forums (CPFs). The CPFs – and subordinate units such as the crime prevention panels (CPPs) and crime prevention committees (CPCs) – "closely conform to structures of customary/traditional leadership ... CPPs and CPCs are analogous with the authority level of Group Village Headman and Village Headman respectively".[165] As such, these new institutions were "portrayed as the reinstatement of traditional peacekeeping structures destroyed under British colonialism and by former President Banda".[166] The incorporation of local governance structures into the community policing model was specifically intended to imbue the undermanned police with greater local legitimacy and extend its reach into communities. As one report noted: "In both urban and rural areas the poor rely on the state police for security and are benefiting from the fact that the MPS and its community policing strategy is utilizing and organizing traditional and customary structures to establish local systems of security and crime prevention."[167] The community policing system established by MALPOD was seized by future initiatives as an effective vehicle to advance community-based approaches to SALW reduction and control, reflecting the natural linkages between SSR and SALW programming.[168]

The Malawi Safety, Security and Justice Project (MaSSAJ) was implemented by DFID to build on the success of MALPOD. Running from 2001 to 2006, it focused on issues of safety, security and justice, including a key emphasis on institutional support to the MPS.[169] Among other activities, MaSSAJ sought to enhance the capacity of the MPS and the Department of Immigration to secure the borders of Malawi and control cross-border flows of SALW.

With funding from Norwegian Aid, the Norwegian Initiative on Small Arms Transfers brought together Norwegian and Malawian non-governmental organizations (NGOs) to implement the Malawi Community Safety, Policing and Firearms Control Programme, which sought to build cooperation at the grassroots level between civil society and the police.[170] One of its key goals was "to address the lack of civilian confidence in the police" that stood as a profound obstacle to SALW reduction and control.[171] The programme, which ran from 1999 to 2001, developed and delivered training for the MPS and over 300 community groups across Malawi. It also produced media and public education campaigns to raise public awareness of the dangers of SALW and promote the need for community policing.[172]

Interestingly, the programme was implemented through the CPFs, which had been established by the MPS with assistance from the DFID-funded MALPOD project. It sought to expand the CPFs and helped to establish community-based police/civil society liaison groups to assist with the implementation of the country's community policing strategy. The overall aim was to "mobilise civil society groups to work in co-operation with the police to monitor and prevent the proliferation of firearms and armed crime and encourage support for better training of police and better accountability to prevent abuse".[173] As one report noted, the programme focused on the need to enhance the community's trust in the MPS so that people would feel comfortable not only in reporting crimes but in sharing information on the illicit trade in SALW in their communities.[174] The programme highlighted the "linkages between tackling small arms proliferation and reforming the security sector" in the Malawian context and beyond.[175]

Lessons learned

SSR and SALW programming in Malawi were linked through a sustained, internationally supported but locally owned police reform programme that had community policing ideas and principles at its core. Early SALW initiatives, such as the Malawi Community Safety, Policing and Firearms Control Programme, made explicit conceptual and programmatic links between the SALW problem and the lack of trust in the MPS. The programme aimed to generate an enabling environment for the community policing model by raising awareness of the dangers posed by SALW proliferation and the role a well-functioning police service can play to counter it. It was a bottom-up effort to rebuild the relationship between citizens and the police, and was an effective complement to the more institutional, top-down reform initiatives supported by MALPOD and MaSSAJ. As one report noted, in Malawi "[SSR] and strengthening is an essential part of addressing the small arms supply issue, as is integrated security sector effort, in tandem with community-based initiatives".[176] The development of community policing in Malawi has been referred to as "one of the greatest successes of SSR programmes in Southern Africa".[177] A particularly notable achievement of the Malawian experience was its development of CPFs to build robust ties between the police and the communities they serve, creating a foundation of social capital upon which SALW programming could thrive. Although it had support from international donors and regional civil society organizations, the Malawian SSR process was largely locally led and driven.[178]

The numbers show that that the Malawian SALW reduction and control process has made significant headway. In its report to the UN Programme of Action on Small Arms and Light Weapons in 2010, the Malawian government outlined progress on several fronts, including the destruction of 1,000 confiscated weapons, the establishment of a firearms registry for legally owned weapons and the marking and registration of illegally owned weapons.[179] Malawi also reported that in 2009 it had established a special commission to review the Firearms Act of 1967,[180] although a 2013 report of the Malawi Human Rights Commission describes the review process as ongoing.[181]

Reflecting the sustainability of Malawi's SSR and SALW programmes, the government's Malawi Police Service Strategic Development Plan 2011–2016 includes detailed targets for a variety of strategic outcomes crucial for long-term SSR and SALW reduction and control efforts, including strengthening the firearms registry by training an additional 100 registry officers, developing a computerized system for the registry and reregistering all legally owned firearms. The government committed to having all community policing structures at station level functional by 2013–2014, and community policing structures and local assembly bodies linked in all communities by 2014–2015. Additionally, it plans to have 13,500 officers trained in both problem solving and the values and principles of community policing by 2015.[182]

The Malawian case shows how, even in resource-constrained environments, well-structured, holistic and integrated SSR and SALW programmes can deliver sustainable progress. Although from a security perspective the Malawian case presented a favourable environment for reform, it nonetheless serves as a model for SSR–SALW integration. The success of the Malawi case stems from the facts that SSR and SALW programming were integrated at all stages of the transition process and programme cycle, and that the process was domestically owned, with donors providing critical funding and technical support. Much can be learned from the Malawi case in the development of future best practices for SSR–SALW integration on the ground in FFCAS. The DRC and Afghanistan, in contrast, represent cautionary examples of how disconnected SSR and SALW programming in unfavourable environments can limit progress and have deleterious and even perverse effects on wider peacebuilding and statebuilding processes.

Partially successful cases

Albania

A political crisis triggered the collapse of Albania's government in 1997. During the riots that followed, military depots across the country were looted of vast quantities of arms, ammunition and explosives, as well as some heavy military equipment. One estimate put the number of weapons stolen at 643,220.[183] In the aftermath of the civil disorder and violence, a sense of insecurity and a lack of confidence in the police persisted among the civilian population. In response, many opted to hold weapons as a means of self-protection.[184] Anxiety over the large quantity of SALW circulating in the country led the Albanian government to request assistance from the UN to recover the weapons.[185] A weapons buy-back scheme was rejected as too costly given the very large number of arms outstanding.[186] The UNDDA instead recommended a community-based approach that offered collective inducements in the form of development projects to encourage voluntary submissions. Altogether, UNDP implemented three weapons collection initiatives from 1998 to 2002, and alongside UNDP's efforts the Albanian government implemented its own arms collection programmes.[187] Undertaken mainly by the Albanian police, with support from local government and civil society actors, these efforts achieved mixed results. Only 15 per cent of the looted weapons were ever recovered, with over 150,000 being smuggled into neighbouring Kosovo to fuel the conflict there.[188]

In addition to a SALW crisis, Albania's police force and the broader security sector were in disarray following the civil strife of 1997. The prevalence of organized crime, human trafficking and corruption made reform efforts especially critical. Moreover, reforming the country's security sector became a strategic priority for Albania as part of its Stabilization and Association Agreement with the EU.[189] A number of SSR initiatives were launched in the wake of the 1997 crisis. The

1998 Constitution placed the intelligence services and police under civil authority and set the stage for further reforms.[190] Albania's initial forays into SSR received external assistance, for instance from the Multinational Advisory Police Element, which was mandated to "advise the Albanian authorities in respect of public order, border control, logistics and communication" and operated from 1997 to 2002.[191]

While this case study focuses most closely UNDP's Support to Security Sector Reform (SSSR) programme – which started in 2003 as a successor to its weapons collections initiatives – other external actors played a significant role in supporting SSR in Albania. The Organization for Security and Co-operation in Europe (OSCE) Mission in Albania provided assistance on security matters and police training, as did the Police Assistance Mission of the European Community to Albania (PAMECA), which began operating in December 2002.[192] Four distinct phases of PAMECA projects have been implemented in Albania, the most recent of which was launched in June 2013 and will continue until October 2016.[193] The US Department of Justice provided support for border management, police training, anti-organized-crime initiatives and governance reforms through its International Criminal Investigative Training Assistance Program.[194] The governments of Denmark and Norway also supported small-scale community police reform projects.[195] In 2013 the Albanian Ministry of Interior implemented "a major restructuring effort to modernize and further professionalize its police service".[196]

Despite these concerted reform efforts, the security sector continues to face major challenges, including problems with internal leadership capacity and a lack of diversity and minority inclusion across the security institutions, particularly pertaining to the country's Roma population.[197] This case study focuses on the relationship between SSR and SALW programmes from the end of the political crisis in 1997 to the conclusion of the UNDP-supported SSSR programme in 2008.

SSR and SALW programming

The Albanian government with support from UNDP, the UN Office for Project Services and the UNDDA launched a community-based weapons collection programme in 1998.[198] Recognizing that SALW control was a key component of broader stabilization and armed violence reduction efforts, the programme combined weapons collection with public works and community development activities.[199] In practice, it focused on a social unit (in this case an Albanian town), providing its inhabitants with the opportunity to turn over their weapons in exchange for development projects benefiting the community.[200] The programme had three main pillars: public awareness raising; the collection and destruction of ordnance; and small-scale community-based development.[201] The pilot project for the scheme was implemented in the district of Gramsh from 1999 to 2000. By the time the pilot was completed, the project had collected 5,981 SALW.[202] The community incentives focused mostly on the development of roads; however, later iterations provided a broad range of development incentives.[203]

The impressive collection results and requests from the general population for access to similar projects led the Albanian government to appeal for community-based weapons collections programmes to be organized in the districts of Elbasan and Diber. This second project, Weapons in Exchange for Development, was implemented from June 2000 to February 2002 and 5,700 weapons were collected.[204] The second project followed the formula of the Gramsh pilot. However, the third UNDP-supported weapons collections programme, the Small Arms and Light Weapons Control Project which ran from April 2002 to December 2003, took a slightly different approach. For the first time, Albanian authorities oversaw all weapons collection and destruction activities. Also, communities collecting weapons had to compete for access to a limited pool of financial resources available for development projects.[205] The local police played a prominent role, working closely with regional coordinators and local groups to help with the collection, recording, removal and storage of surrendered weapons. The collected SALW were subsequently handed over to the armed forces.[206] UNDP estimated that within the framework of the project, 8,500 weapons were collected at a cost of about US$404 per weapon.[207] Taken together, UNDP's three community-based SALW collection programmes brought in 20,181 SALW at a total cost of roughly US$8 million.[208] Two external factors complicated weapons collection activities. First, a large number of the looted weapons likely ended up in Kosovo due to the conflict in 1998–1999. Second, the Albanian government's failure to legislate a limit on the amnesty provided to holders of SALW undermined the urgency of collection initiatives.

The failings of Albania's security sector likewise posed a challenge to SALW control programming. A 2005 Saferworld report stressed that a lack of trust in the security sector was not conducive to voluntary weapons collection.[209] At the time, opinion polls indicated a low level of trust in state bodies, particularly law enforcement and justice institutions. The Saferworld report, which featured extensive focus group research, noted that as long as there continued to be a lack of trust in state officials and authorities, citizens would be reluctant to surrender their weapons.[210] More than half of those surveyed believed that levels of security and stability needed to improve before they would consider surrendering their illegally held firearms, illustrating the connection between security institutions, public confidence and SALW control.[211]

In 2003 UNDP decided to shift the focus of its intervention from SALW collection to supporting security sector transformation and governance, launching the SSSR programme. More specifically, it opted to focus on micro-level initiatives to foster the development of community policing in Albania. The programme was explicitly designed to leverage the established network of local contacts UNDP had developed through its SALW projects. The goal was to use these relationships, the SALW projects' positive reputation and the considerable local knowledge generated as an entry point for SSR.[212] The UNDP SSSR programme was a grassroots community policing initiative that ran from 2003 to 2008 and aimed to "improve public order at the local level, strengthen police capacities, [and] promote a positive police image and the role of the police as a provider of public services".[213] It sought to achieve "quick wins to demonstrate the advantages of close collaboration and teamwork between the police and the public, to build mutual trust and respect towards effective crime prevention and conflict resolution in the community".[214]

The SSSR programme had three pillars: a public awareness campaign and community interaction initiative intended to improve the image of the police; the establishment of community problem-solving groups of community members, responsible for liaising with the police on safety and security issues; and an information campaign targeting schools that gave police access to classrooms to discuss public safety issues such as drugs, weapons, crime and alcohol abuse.[215] As one DCAF workshop report noted:

> [F]or the UNDP, an initial involvement with a SALW project in Albania was later expanded into a more comprehensive framework of assistance in the area of Security Sector Reform. These different approaches to SSR underscore that the concept can be operational in both theory and in practice.[216]

Initial evaluations were positive about UNDP's transition from a SALW reduction and control programme to community-based SSR constructed on an understanding that the community policing model was most likely to take root "from below".[217] Because the SSSR programme was based on leveraging relationships developed at the local level during the SALW process and generating local capacity to engage with the police, it was expressly designed to operate at the local level and paid limited attention to national-level policy processes and reforms. Later evaluations were critical of this approach, doubting how much effect these local-level interventions had in influencing policing policy at the national level.[218] Other reports questioned the commitment of the Albanian authorities to the concept of community policing altogether, and indicated that as of 2009 Albania's leadership still saw community policing as a "luxury" for a police force that struggled to perform basic functions.[219] Although the national-level impact of UNDP's SSSR programme was unclear when it ceased operation in 2008, the Albanian government has since demonstrated a strong commitment to the community policing concept.[220]

Lessons learned

As in many FFCAS, the link between SSR and SALW in Albania revolved around the issue of public confidence in the state's ability to provide safety and security to the general public. Both the Albanian government and major external donors recognized that the long-term viability of SALW control would be dependent to a certain degree on effective SSR programming, particularly in the area of policing, which could help to build trust in the capacity of the security institutions. The SSR and SALW programmes unfolded sequentially rather than simultaneously, meaning there was limited opportunity for mutually beneficial joint programming. However, the success of SALW programming certainly carved out an entry point for SSR, exemplified by UNDP's pivot from SALW control to community policing initiatives. UNDP's experience in Albania demonstrated the momentum the two processes can create for each other if appropriately aligned.

Despite significant gains made by the SALW and SSR programmes at the community level, they initially struggled to drive sustainable change at the national level. The UNDP programme focused on local initiatives to facilitate community policing, but these efforts were somewhat detached from national-level reform processes. However, by 2010 community policing was adopted as a core element of the Albanian government's police reform process, sustained by donor support from a variety of actors including the OSCE and the Swedish International Development Agency (SIDA).[221] The Albanian government has shown growing ownership of the community policing concept, establishing the 2011–2013 Community Policing Action Plan and committing itself to a multiyear reform programme in partnership with SIDA.[222] Though they were not directly integrated, the gains made by the community policing programmes can be partially attributed to the legacy of early SALW initiatives, which provided a foundation of community relationships, local knowledge and institutional legitimacy for SSR. The Albanian case represents partial success in SSR–SALW integration, in that locally owned SALW programming paved the way for SSR. Opportunities may have been missed in the early stage of the transition to launch SSR activities that could simultaneously buttress and expand SALW programming, but the case nonetheless shows the benefits that can be accrued by forming even sequential SSR–SALW linkages.

Cambodia

After 30 years of war, conflict and genocide, Cambodia in 1998 was an unstable and fragile state awash with SALW. Although in the aftermath of the 1991 peace agreement the UN Transitional Authority in Cambodia administered a weapons collection programme – which ran from 1992 to 1993 – by the mid-1990s the UN estimated that over 500,000 SALW and 80 million rounds of ammunition remained in circulation.[223] In spite of the early disarmament efforts, the continuing threat of the Khmer Rouge and the lack of public trust in the government's ability to provide security meant that many communities held on to weapons for self-defence.[224] The Cambodian government and its international partners saw this accumulation of SALW in the hands of individuals and non-state groups as a threat to the country's stability and prospects for continuing peace. To counter the proliferation of SALW, the Cambodian government launched a domestic weapons collection programme in 1998 that also banned private ownership of weapons. The programme targeted illegal weapons located inside the capital city of Phnom Penh and gave provincial leaders a mandate to undertake their own weapons collection operations, with the promise of money or food in exchange for weapons.[225]

More than 100,000 weapons were collected by the programme, which continued until the Cambodian government ran out of money to support it.[226] In response to Cambodian government requests for donor assistance to address the SALW problem further, the EU launched the EU Assistance on Curbing Small Arms and Light Weapons in Cambodia (EU-ASAC) programme in April 2000. Three years later the government of Japan – which had also been a key funder of EU-ASAC – launched the Japan Assistance Team for Small Arms Management in Cambodia (JSAC), a programme with similar goals.

Adding to the difficulty of SALW collection, Cambodia's security sector was oversized, unprofessional and in serious need of reform. As one report noted, the armed forces often "compound[ed] rather than mitigate[d] security problems, particularly in Cambodia's rural areas".[227] Another report noted that one of the major challenges facing the Cambodian government's SALW collection programme was the "inability of the Cambodian security forces (police, gendarmerie, and army) to ensure internal security and uphold the rule of law".[228] In spite of the clear deficiencies of the security sector, the security forces – mainly the military – accounted for approximately 40 per cent of government spending.[229] International donors, in particular the World Bank, identified the size and fiscal unsustainability of the armed forces as a key reform priority, choosing to fund an aggressive military downsizing programme.[230]

Both EU-ASAC and later JSAC identified political instability and public perceptions of insecurity as key impediments to the voluntary collection of weapons which formed the core of the SALW agenda. Consequently, both programmes recognized that progress in SALW reduction and control was dependent to a certain degree on improvements in the professionalism of the security forces. The Cambodian population had to be reassured that they no longer required weapons for self-defence. Both programmes made a strong policy and programmatic link between SALW goals, such as reducing the number of weapons in circulation and improving the stockpile management and weapons destruction capabilities of the armed forces, and SSR imperatives, such as training the police and improving the relationship between the police and society. As in Albania, initial SALW reduction and control activities provided an entry point for SSR programming. However, despite some early gains, the country's SSR process eventually stalled. A series of *ad hoc* and interim SSR projects, many directly linked to SALW initiatives, did not evolve into a comprehensive and holistic SSR programme. Critics later argued that the imperative to downsize the military dominated the combined SSR–DDR agenda in Cambodia at the expense of broader issues of governance, transparency and accountability.[231]

SSR and SALW programming

After conducting an initial needs assessment, EU-ASAC found that Cambodia's security situation was marked not only by the large numbers of weapons held by the civilian population, but also a "lack of professional ability on the part of law and order institutions".[232] These failings contributed not only to high levels of violence and a lack of economic development but also to a lack of trust between society and the security sector. To make progress on several fronts, EU-ASAC endeavoured to combine SSR and SALW programming. Increasing the professional capacity of the police and improving police–community relations were prioritized, along with efforts to remove weapons from circulation, reduce weapons-related violence and crime and support local weapons-for-development projects.[233]

In April 2003 JSAC officially began operating and launched its Peace Building and Comprehensive Small Arms Management Programme in Cambodia. The programme had five component projects: weapons reduction and development for peace; safe storage and registration; weapons destruction; public awareness; and National Commission support.[234] The JSAC programme, which ran until April 2008, was rooted, like EU-ASAC, in the notion that SSR and SALW programming were inextricably linked.

Weapons-for-development schemes were a core part of EU-ASAC and JSAC. Between 2001 and 2003 EU-ASAC supported infrastructure projects – at first through direct funding, later through the participation of local NGOs and finally through government agencies – in areas where significant numbers of SALW had been collected. At the same time, the programme in conjunction with local NGO partners worked to raise awareness of SALW issues.[235] Local NGOs were integrated into EU-ASAC programming, for instance by cooperating with the police to record weapons collected.[236] Evaluations of these interventions tended to be positive. Surveys in villages hosting EU-ASAC projects found both improved perceptions of security and diminished concerns about arms-related violence.[237] Like EU-ASAC, JSAC spearheaded voluntary weapons collection and destruction initiatives, and offered development projects in exchange for weapons surrendered by communities.[238] JSAC also organized awareness activities to educate the public, government officials and members of the security sector on the dangers associated with weapons possession and proliferation, all with an eye to encouraging public participation in the programme.[239]

Collectively, the programmes significantly reduced the number of SALW outside state control and succeeded in greatly lowering the level of crime and armed violence in the country. By 2006 45 storage facilities had been built and 142,871 weapons destroyed by EU-ASAC.[240] For its part, JSAC had collected 30,360 weapons and 118,689 rounds of ammunition and explosives by the end of its mandate in 2008.[241] It is estimated that there were 400,000–500,000 SALW circulating in Cambodia in the 1990s.[242] The collaboration between external donors, the Cambodian government and NGOs resulted in the collection of 207,000 weapons by 2007.[243] An evaluation of the EU-ASAC programme found that as of 1991 82 per cent of weapons in the country had been brought under government control, while between 1998 and 2003 armed violence fell by 70 per cent and the homicide rate dropped by 50 per cent.[244]

In tandem with their SALW control and stockpile management initiatives, both EU-ASAC and JSAC included police reform as an integral element of their programming. An EU-ASAC project document recognized that "increasing local confidence in the ability of the security forces is ... vital".[245] Among the topics of police training courses provided by EU-ASAC in 1999 were human rights and community relations. By improving police capacity to engage communities in a constructive and rights-respecting fashion, the programme aimed to build public trust in the state security sector and, by extension, SALW reduction and control efforts.[246] EU-ASAC also provided entrepreneurial training to police officers' wives to develop their ability to generate an income, hoping to counter endemic corruption driven by low police salaries.[247] In 2002 EU-ASAC supported the development of a training curriculum and training manuals for community police officers in conjunction with representatives from the training department of the national police, the Working Group for Weapons Reduction and national human rights NGOs. This collaboration between government and civil society bolstered vital state–society trust and social capital.[248] In 2003 police in several provinces participated in a two-week training course based on this curriculum, and the training manuals are now used by the training department of the national police.[249] Overall, evaluations of EU-ASAC programming found improvements in public perceptions of the general security situation and the police force's competence to manage it, a testament to the legacy of the training and infrastructure built.[250]

SSR and SALW activities were similarly integrated under the auspices of JSAC programming. JSAC drew the same conclusion about the connection between police performance, the public's perception of threat and the demand for SALW. On the role of police training, JSAC project documents argued that police support and training was intended to "improve security and create an environment that the residents can believe that they no longer need weapons for their self protection".[251] The aim of the JSAC training was "to improve the capacity and the level of awareness of the police officers, and thus improve public relations and community security", with the expected outcome that improved police performance would "encourage citizens to dismiss weapons as a necessary means of self-defence ... therefore further promoting weapons surrender".[252] To develop such synergies between police reform and SALW reduction and control programming, JSAC held workshops and seminars in 2007 to educate the police, media, public officials, the armed forces and the general public on the Law on Weapons, Explosives and Ammunition Management, which entered into force in May 2005.[253] JSAC also contributed to capacity building of the police force through training, provision of materials and strengthening stockpile management systems.[254] When JSAC completed its police training programme in January 2007 it had trained a total of 454 police officers.

EU-ASAC and JSAC SALW projects often required the collaboration of the security forces, as both the police and the armed forces took part in the voluntary weapons collection and destruction work.[255] Secure storage facilities and a weapons register for the police and military emerged from the capacity-building efforts. Surplus weapons were destroyed, while the remainder were securely stored to curtail the possibility of leakage.[256] When EU-ASAC concluded its operations in 2006, all SALW held by the Ministry of National Defence had been registered and securely stored, with 45 storage depots built or renovated and 3,475 lockable weapons storage racks installed in offices and barracks.[257] JSAC similarly built safe storage facilities and provided training and registration assistance for police weapons stores.[258]

EU-ASAC consistently encouraged cooperation between the security sector, the community and government officials at various levels.[259] The projects also facilitated the participation of civil society and parliament in their legislative reform components.[260] EU-ASAC offered legal support that contributed to the alteration of the existing legislation and legal framework regarding SALW.[261] The Law on the Management of Weapons, Explosives and Ammunition placed greater restrictions on private ownership of guns while imposing harsher punishment for crimes involving guns.[262] The EU-ASAC project manager noted in a report that the positive impacts of the weapons collection projects were strengthened by capacity-building initiatives targeting the security sector.[263]

Summary of connections between SSR and SALW in EU-ASAC programming

1. EU-ASAC included the security forces in weapons collection and destruction programmes, "insisting on appropriate cooperation between relevant police and military forces and local and national authorities, and building community-security sector relationships".

2. EU-ASAC supported "wide social and parliamentary engagement with arms law reform".

3. EU-ASAC programming explicitly aimed "to increase public trust in protection by police forces".

4. EU-ASAC "supported the registration and safe storage of weapons stocks by the military (Ministry of National Defence) and the National Police".

Source: Mike Bourne and Owen Greene, "Armed violence, governance, security sector reform, and safety, security and access to justice", briefing paper, Centre for International Cooperation and Security, Bradford, 2014, p. 6.

Lessons learned

The positive impact of SALW initiatives on Cambodia's SSR process in its early stages is clear, most prominently in the contribution they made to stabilizing the fragile post-conflict environment. SALW programming helped re-establish a monopoly on force and created a permissive security environment for SSR.[264] SSR, for its part, was aimed at restoring public trust in the state security sector and consolidating the weapons control gains made by SALW programming. SSR and SALW were, in the context of EU-ASAC and JSAC programming, mutually enabling.

There are two important lessons to take away from the experience of SSR and SALW programming in Cambodia in the period 1998–2006. First, integrated SSR–SALW programming was able to build trust between the Cambodian public and the police while reducing the likelihood of a return to violence. These achievements came at a volatile time in Cambodia's transition, and contributed to the country's stabilization.

Second, while the success of SALW programming provided entry points for SSR programming, a holistic, governance-focused SSR agenda never materialized. In its initial years the SSR process was overly concentrated on right-sizing the armed forces at the expense of other key reform targets. For instance, the lack of attention paid to the governance dimensions of the SSR agenda threatened the gains made by SALW programming. Effective SALW control regimes require robust and accountable governance mechanisms to oversee them over the long term. As one 2014 report noted, Cambodia continues to suffer from "a gap between security providing institutions (armed forces, police, military police) and security oversight institutions (national assembly and senate, judiciary, civil society organizations)" and low levels of trust between the general public and the armed forces.[265] Further illustrating governance problems within the security sector, the armed forces have been accused of abuses of power, human rights violations and politically motivated killings, most recently following the July 2013 elections when the army was involved in the harsh repression of political unrest.[266] The failure of SSR to address adequately problems of corruption, clientelism and abuses of power through systematic governance reforms has placed the significant achievements of the SALW programme at risk. Growing public distrust in the security forces could roll back the SALW gains. In this sense the Cambodian case, like that of Albania, could be considered a partial success. SSR–SALW programmatic connections gave a boost to both SSR and SALW activities early in the transition, but did not generate the type of long-term integrated programming that could definitively consolidate those gains.

El Salvador

During the 1970s and 1980s weapons poured into Central America from a variety of sources, mainly as a result of Cold War conflicts.[267] These weapons fuelled El Salvador's 12-year civil war, which claimed the lives of roughly 75,000 people.[268] The 1992 peace agreement that ended the conflict contained robust provisions on DDR and SSR, implicitly linking the two projects. Security sector transformation was a core demand of the Farabundo Marti National Liberation Front (FMLN) guerrilla group and was fundamental to the peace process. The agreement laid the groundwork for reforms of the armed forces, police, justice system and intelligence services. In the years following the peace agreement, major milestones were achieved, including the DDR of former combatants, the transformation of the FMLN into a political party and the creation of a new police force. The government honoured its commitments to military downsizing and the removal of officials implicated in major human rights abuses. Over time, the country experienced a demilitarization of politics and the entrenchment of civilian control over the security sector. Most importantly, there were no violations of the ceasefire and ultimately no resumption of political violence.

The successes achieved in DDR and SSR under the auspices of the peace agreement were not matched by progress in SALW reduction and control, despite the widespread proliferation of illicit weapons. The civil war left behind hundreds of thousands of weapons in the hands of the civilian population, including everything from rifles and handguns to grenades.[269] Weapons flows continued unabated in the post-civil war period, fuelling a wave of gang-related criminal violence that gave El Salvador one of the world's highest homicide rates.[270] By 2005 80 per cent of homicides in the country were committed with firearms.[271] Ultimately, this has led to a deep sense of public insecurity. In response, the government has pursued an aggressive and repressive public security strategy, which has raised concerns about the re-emergence of militarized policing and backsliding on commitments to human rights. In this environment, it is perhaps unsurprising that SALW reduction and control policies have yet to gain serious traction.[272] El Salvador's justice sector and penal system are in crisis, leaving serious gaps in the society's rule of law framework. On a more general level, SALW control efforts are complicated by the prominent role of firearms in Salvadoran society, where gun possession is considered in some quarters as a fundamental right.[273]

SSR and SALW programming

Under the peace agreement the government pledged to subject its security and justice institutions to a series of reforms in exchange for the FMLN agreeing to disarm. As a senior FMLN negotiator put it: "the FMLN was willing to engage in politics without arms and to accept that the official armed forces kept arms without engaging in politics".[274] The first disarmament of FMLN and government forces started in June 1992,[275] with the UN Observer Mission in El Salvador (ONUSAL) monitoring search-and-destroy missions for weapons caches belonging to the FMLN. More than 11,000 FMLN fighters surrendered some 10,200 SALW and 9,200 grenades.[276] While these weapons were destroyed, those belonging to government forces were collected and stored.[277] However, the peace agreement deliberately chose to put aside broader SALW challenges in order to make progress on the FMLN's main area of concern, the reform of the country's security sector. The country transitioned immediately from a large-scale, state-supported disarmament process aimed at the warring parties and designed to consolidate political stability to a limited set of voluntary weapons collection activities largely driven by civil society groups and international agencies. Despite the presence of hundreds of thousands of uncontrolled weapons in the country, either unsecured in government depots or in civilian hands, a large-scale SALW programme was not seen as politically viable or desirable at the time. In effect, the process "side-stepped the challenge of reducing and regulating civilian possession of firearms".[278]

Key initiatives of the voluntary weapons collection phase included the Goods for Guns programme, implemented from September 1996 to June 1999. Goods for Guns was an initiative of the Patriotic Movement against Crime, a coalition of citizens, businesses, NGOs and churches. In return for vouchers for consumer goods, the programme collected a total of 9,527 weapons and 129,696 rounds of ammunition.[279] In 2000, with technical and financial assistance from UNDP's Emergency Response Division, the UNDP country office in El Salvador launched the Strengthening Mechanisms for Small Arms Control project,[280] the first UN-sponsored SALW-related initiative in El Salvador since the end of the civil war. Another UNDP initiative, the Arms-Free Municipalities project, involved a municipal-level ban on carrying firearms in public spaces combined with enforcement by the national police, who were empowered to administer fines and confiscate weapons. These programmes were first adopted on a pilot basis in a handful of cities and showed promising results – including a 49 per cent reduction in the homicide rate and a 24 per cent drop in crimes committed with firearms[281] – and subsequently expanded to 30 cities across the country. However, as one author noted, when the SALW control activities were launched, "the commitment to living in a disarmed society" did not exist.[282]

In spite of these SALW collection efforts, in 2001 estimates put the number of military-grade weapons circulating in the civilian population at 360,000.[283] The Salvadoran government and FMLN mainly conceded that in the years following the peace accords a large number of weapons would remain in civilian hands. The failure to address SALW control efforts as part of the peace process meant that even with peace the society remained militarized. The subsequent rise in organized crime challenged the ability of the police to provide public order and security, which made it exceedingly difficult to undertake voluntary disarmament initiatives.

DDR projects undertaken in the first years following the peace agreement were ineffective, leaving many combatants from both sides of the conflict unemployed, with few valuable skills. Many of these young men turned to organized crime groups to meet their needs. This situation, combined with the ready availability of SALW, fuelled rampant gang-related violence. As of 2011, 70 per cent of homicides were committed with a firearm, compared to a global average of 42 per cent.[284] According to law enforcement estimates in 2012, there are 27,000 members of the Mara Salvatrucha (MS-13) and Barrio 18 gangs on the streets in El Salvador, and another 9,000 in prisons.[285]

El Salvador's civil war saw grave human rights violations perpetrated by both parties to the conflict. To satisfy the demands of the FMLN, the peace agreement included three sweeping military reforms: a reduction in the size of the army, a redefinition of its mission away from domestic law enforcement and the purging of officials most responsible for human rights abuses.[286] The goal of a reduction in the size of the military was quickly met, with the armed forces decreasing from 63,175 in January 1992 to 31,000 in February 1993 and 15,000 by the mid-2000s.[287] The military retreated from political life and submitted to civilian authority and oversight. The peace agreement called for the dismissal of the military and treasury police and their replacement with an integrated, newly trained National Civil Police (PNC), made up of 60 per cent new recruits, 20 per cent former police and 20 per cent opposition combatants.[288] The PNC's establishment signalled the reorientation of the military away from domestic security concerns. The speed and success of this crucial restructuring of the country's security sector were a major factor in the maintenance of post-conflict peace.

One of the key challenges in police reform in El Salvador was developing a new rights-respecting police force that could simultaneously play a role in shepherding and safeguarding the war-to-peace transition. International donors helped the PNC to cultivate expertise on weapons tracing, seizure and collection as well as destruction techniques.[289] UNDP and the Office of the UN High Commissioner for Human Rights (OHCHR) "focused on training, creating modules and helping local police leadership develop police doctrine".[290] With the assistance of UNDP and the OHCHR, pivotal documents, protocols and procedures were created for the new police, including a code of conduct, operating procedures for various specialist police divisions (including the border police, ports and airports police and public order or "riot" police) and citizen complaint forms for alleged police misconduct.[291] By January 1997 the PNC had succeeded in improving security in urban marketplaces and public transportation, which were two major areas where weapons, especially hand grenades, were being used.[292] A decade after the signing of the peace accords, police reform was widely considered a success in El Salvador, with one adviser to ONUSAL noting that "the new force had been created in two years and had a distinct 'civilian character'".[293] However, as time passed it became increasingly clear that the PNC lacked the capability to address the rapid expansion of organized crime enabled by the ready availability of SALW.

Lessons learned

The initial years following the 1992 peace accord in El Salvador saw promising synergies develop between SSR, DDR and SALW programming, which were core elements of the peace accord. However, after early progress, durable linkages between SSR and long-term SALW programming did not evolve. Despite the widespread availability of illicit SALW, there was little political will to advance a comprehensive SALW reduction and control initiative. The ready availability of SALW and their associated role in gang-fuelled criminality had the effect of slowly rolling back the substantial achievements made in SSR, notably the democratization and demilitarization of policing. The failure to integrate SSR and SALW programming not only facilitated growing insecurity but contributed to the reversal of some gains made in entrenching human rights norms and good governance principles in the country's security institutions.

The first decade following the peace accord was characterized by successful SSR, including the establishment of civilian oversight and control mechanisms and the demilitarization of politics. Donors chose to focus on strengthening institutional capacity and governance mechanisms in the security sector first, only later turning their attention to the threats of organized crime and community violence.[294] As one critic noted, "though El Salvador's transition has successfully dismantled or subordinated the institutions most responsible for human rights violations during the armed conflict, it has largely failed to create lawful and effective agencies in their stead".[295] Reports in 2012 found that "despite numerous attempts at police reform, the civilian security forces created to replace the military as the guardians of public order remain riddled with corruption and have been penetrated by organized crime and gangs".[296] Efforts to prosecute arrested gang members are often hampered by police corruption. From a justice perspective, "inefficiency and corruption continue to plague the court system. Salvadoran police and prosecutors often find it difficult to coordinate efforts, and relatively few arrests lead to successful prosecutions as a result".[297] Unsurprisingly, a 2016 report noted that the country had a paltry criminal conviction rate of 5 per cent.[298]

Partly as a result of these failings, the second decade after the peace accord has been dominated by an epidemic of gang-related violence. In response, the state adopted a largely repressive security policy (known as "Iron Fist" or "Mano Dura") to combat organized crime. It gave the police sweeping powers of arrest: suspected gang members could be arrested merely for having gang tattoos or associating with gang members.[299] These controversial tactics have been criticized for stigmatizing poor communities, increasing resentment of the military and police and, according to one study, accelerating gang recruitment.[300] From a policing perspective, the strategy seriously undermined the community policing system that formed the bedrock of the police force. Instead, "misconduct, arbitrary detention and excessive use of force continue to present major obstacles to the establishment of a professional police force in the country ... [with] more than 8 per cent of Salvadorans saying they had been victims of police abuse in the past year".[301]

Observers fear that the inability of the police force to control gang-related violence will lead the army to "once again take the lead in law enforcement".[302] According to one report, "the country has opted to hand the reins to the institution best-known to provide order: the military".[303] As one UN report noted, in 2012 the Salvadoran government "replaced the entire command staff of their police force with career military officers".[304]

In 2015 there were 7,000 military troops undertaking domestic law enforcement operations.[305] The military's re-entry into domestic policing was facilitated by former President Funes's 2009 decree – challenged and upheld by the country's Supreme Court in 2014 – that gave the military explicit authority to undertake police functions.[306] In El Salvador, where roughly half (51 per cent) of respondents to a 2013 public opinion survey said they were "afraid to walk alone at night within a kilometer of their home", the appeal of authoritarian and military responses to crime is obvious.[307] In this sense, "crime has become a direct threat to democratic governance".[308]

The El Salvador case illustrates both the tremendous potential of SSR–SALW integration to deliver positive outcomes and how the breakdown of that integration can undermine broader peacebuilding and statebuilding objectives. In the initial years after the peace accord, strong links between SSR and SALW programming paid major public security dividends. Locally owned SSR and SALW processes succeeded in demilitarizing both the FMLN and the government security forces according to democratic norms and principles, and transformed the police into an effective and rights-respecting body. However, the lack of political will to maintain the momentum of early SSR and DDR programming with a comprehensive SALW reduction and control initiative gradually reversed many of the gains made, facilitating a sharp rise in criminality. The notion, supported by some El Salvadorian reformers, that SSR could be advanced while the problem of widespread SALW proliferation continued unabated proved to be faulty. The subsequent remilitarization of the security sector has exemplified the need to advance SSR and SALW in an integrated and mutually reinforcing manner.

Failed cases

Democratic Republic of the Congo

Even though the DRC is typically viewed as a post-conflict state, armed violence within the country remains habitual and widespread.[309] Local and foreign armed groups have perpetuated a cycle of violence that has resulted in over 5.4 million deaths, 2.7 million internally displaced persons, widespread sexual violence and massive violations of human rights and international law.[310] The country's eastern region remains plagued by conflict and the uncontrolled circulation and use of SALW.[311] SALW proliferation in the DRC has been driven by various factors, including persistent armed conflict, the unlawful extraction of natural resources, porous borders and entrenched poverty and inequality.[312] The flow of weapons into the country has contributed to atrocious human rights abuses and stymied economic and human development.[313] It has been estimated that civilians in eastern DRC alone possess at least 300,000 weapons.[314]

In 2003 an arms embargo on the DRC was introduced due to unrelenting violence in the regions of North and South Kivu and Ituri. It aimed to block arms supplies and military support to militant groups in the conflict-affected areas.[315] In 2005 the embargo was expanded nationwide with several exemptions, including weapons supplies earmarked for the Congolese army and police force.[316] Although consistently renewed, the embargo has largely failed to put a stop to the trafficking of SALW in the DRC.[317] The supply of weapons and ammunition to the Congolese armed forces from international sources such as China, Ukraine, France, South Africa, Egypt, Zimbabwe and the United States has been a major driver of SALW proliferation.[318] Leakage of SALW from army stockpiles is frequently cited as a main source of weapons for the DRC's armed groups.[319] Poor stockpile management, a culture of impunity, endemic corruption and low or nonexistent salaries for some soldiers have all contributed to the diversion of official weapons.[320] Indeed, reports show that armed groups, especially the Congrès national pour la défense du peuple, have acquired weapons and ammunition from the army, the Forces Armées de la République Démocratique du Congo (FARDC), by purchasing, stealing or seizing them by force.[321] The UN has also reported that regional states such as Rwanda and Uganda have supplied weapons directly to rebel groups within the DRC.[322]

SSR, DDR and SALW programming

SSR and DDR programming in the DRC have been and remain poorly integrated. Between 2002 and 2009 the World Bank's Multi-Country Demobilization and Reintegration Programme (MDRP) attempted to stabilize the Great Lakes region of Africa by supporting DDR in seven countries, including the DRC.[323] Notably, the MDRP disbursed US$272 million to finance the Programme National de Désarmement, Démobilisation et Réinsertion launched in 2004, in addition to six special projects mainly aimed at demobilizing child soldiers.[324] In principle, ex-combatants had to possess a weapon or a certificate of disarmament to access the reintegration benefits of the programme.[325] Functional weapons collected through the programme were handed in to the FARDC, while faulty weapons and heavy armaments were destroyed.[326] The national programme in the DRC ended in 2009, and resulted in the collection of 118,558 weapons and the demobilization of 102,104 former combatants.[327]

In 2003 the UN Organization Mission in the DRC (MONUC)[328] was mandated to assist in the DDR process, which led to the creation of two programmes: the Spontaneous Voluntary Disarmament Programme, implemented in collaboration with the MDRP,[329] and the Disarmament and Community Reinsertion Programme, executed with the support of UNDP. The latter resulted in the demobilization of 19,394 combatants and the collection of more than 11,403 weapons as well as a considerable amount of ammunition, grenades and landmines.[330] MONUC also undertook a DDR, repatriation and resettlement (DDR-RR) programme that focused on foreign militias.[331] Between 2002 and 2011 MONUC repatriated more than 14,172 foreign soldiers and 9,834 dependants.[332]

In May 2005 the Congolese government adopted the Plan National Stratégique pour l'Intégration des Forces armées, which sought to reintegrate former rebels into the army.[333] One report notes that the plan had the effect of creating a "divided and weak army, where multiple parallel networks and personal connections ... inflated ranks and lowered combat capability".[334] According to Hoffman, the army reintegration mandated by the plan "was intended to break down old wartime loyalties and replace them with a unified chain of command. But in many cases different factions remained in control of their former units and competed over the distribution of lucrative posts and deployment in resourceful areas."[335] The infrequent and insufficient pay provided to the state security services pushed them to "demand unofficial fees and taxes for their security services" and made them part "of the logic of privatised and partisan security provision, which further decreased the legitimacy of the state".[336] Flawed DDR policies, which sowed sentiments of disunity and disenfranchisement in the Congolese army, undercut the SSR process and contributed to corruption-driven SALW diversion.

Comprehensive SSR was intended to take place after the completion of DDR in the DRC.[337] DDR was perceived as launching pad for the creation of a new army that could stabilize the conflict-affected eastern region.[338] The setbacks encountered by the DDR process, however, meant that SSR would be advanced on a parallel and largely separate track to DDR.[339]

The development of the latest iteration of DDR in the DRC, dubbed DDR III and launched after the FARDC's defeat of the M23 rebel group in November 2013, targeted the M23 and a range of other rebel groups in eastern Congo.[340] There is a broad awareness of the need to correct previous DDR errors to preserve a chance for peace: "National DDR programmes in the past have failed due to the lack of resources and political will, duration of programme implementation time, failure to effectively sensitize armed groups and communities, and failures to properly reintegrate ex-combatants into the military or provide alternative livelihoods."[341] The DDR III strategy has several steps: the sensitization of armed groups; the disarmament and encampment of armed groups; the provision of demobilization assistance with biometric identification; medical screening and vetting; and the selection of reintegration options, including military integration, with the assistance of reintegration preparatory centres.[342] With US$100 million in funds from various donors and multilateral agencies as well as the UN Organization Stabilization Mission in the Democratic Republic of the Congo (as MONUC was renamed), the programme aims to reintegrate 11,785 ex-combatants from over 50 armed groups, including 1,800 M23 ex-fighters.[343] As of mid-2015, this new DDR initiative has not been effectively integrated with ongoing SSR programming, with the links between the two blurry at best.[344]

SALW reduction and control activities have likewise not been integrated with SSR programming in the DRC, despite the launch of a series of SALW initiatives in different areas of the country with the support of NGOs, the Congolese government and external donors. In 2005 the Congolese NGO Programme oecuménique de paix, transformation des conflits et réconciliation (PAREC) launched a voluntary SALW collection programme where weapons were exchanged for bicycles and other necessities.[345] It resulted in the collection of 9,565 weapons.[346] From November 2008 to May 2009 PAREC implemented a weapons buyback programme in Kinshasa where each weapon was exchanged for US$100.[347] The programme collected 12,090 weapons and other military items such as explosives, uniforms and daggers.[348] Overall, close to 22,000 weapons were collected by PAREC between 2005 and 2009 and turned over to the Congolese government.[349] In March 2014 the government, with the support of UNDP, launched its first voluntary civilian disarmament operation in Ituri. This weapons-for-development scheme was allocated a budget of US$400,000 with the aim of collecting 2,500 SALW.[350] When the operation ended in August 2014, more than 11,000 SALW had been collected.[351]

Despite some modest gains made in DDR and SALW reduction and control programmes, the Congolese government's inability to control weapons stockpiles has undercut their long-term impact. Research from the UN Group of Experts has shown that government stockpiles are an important source of weapons and ammunition for armed groups in the DRC.[352] Significant numbers of civilians and members of rebel groups have been apprehended with government-issued SALW.[353] In addition to finding military supplies in local markets, former members of armed groups have confirmed that they repeatedly purchased weapons, ammunition and uniforms directly from the Congolese army.[354]

In spite of the DRC being a signatory of the Nairobi Protocol, the government did not, as of 2015, have proper safeguards to prevent the leakage of legal weapons and ammunition, with the UN Security Council urging the government to implement a national weapons marking programme.[355] Currently, state-owned SALW are neither uniformly marked nor properly registered.[356] In 2010 three marking machines were donated to the Congolese government, which planned to mark 250,000 weapons from its stockpile of 2 million weapons within five years.[357] However, it was not until December 2014 that the government carried out its first weapons marking programme in Bunia.[358] With UNDP support, the initiative resulted in the collection and screening of 692 arms, of which 550 were electronically marked.[359] This positive step merely highlighted the urgent need for the Congolese government to implement a national weapons marking programme and produce a detailed record of its security forces' weapons and ammunition.[360] As of 2011, the DRC had neither a centralized record-keeping system nor a national electronic database to monitor SALW.[361] This lack of a monitoring and regulatory system has contributed to the diversion of state-owned weapons and ammunition. The failure to link SALW and DDR activities with efforts to build stockpile management capacity under the auspices of SSR has set back broader reform and stabilization efforts.

Since April 2003 international donors have devoted extensive resources to SSR in the DRC, with little concrete progress.[362] The DRC's security sector continues to be a source of predation rather than protection for the civilian population. Overall, SSR programming has been focused on tackling short-term crises such as violence in the east, while overlooking longer-term governance reforms.[363] Most importantly, SSR in the DRC is characterized by a lack of local ownership.[364] Donors have encouraged a holistic approach to reform, while the Congolese government has remained chiefly concerned with constructing an operationally effective army.[365] The strategies are not necessarily incompatible, but have not been harmonized within the SSR agenda.[366] Despite the defeat of the M23 and the signing of the February 2014 Peace, Security and Cooperation Framework that has bound the DRC's neighbours and regional powers to cease all proxy competition in the country and assist the DRC government to promote peace and stability, scant progress has been made on SSR. As Wilén writes, despite the Congolese government's pronouncements on SSR, "structural reforms and an overarching SSR roadmap are still items on the 'to-do' list".[367]

Lessons learned

The experience of SSR and SALW integration in the DRC has been characterized by missed opportunities. Perhaps the best example of this is the ongoing failure of the FARDC to implement stockpile management reforms, which has undermined modest success in SALW collection. DDR and DDR-RR programming in the DRC have resulted in a considerable number of weapons collected from non-state armed groups; likewise, SALW collection initiatives undertaken by local NGOs, and later UNDP, have collected a substantial number of SALW from the civilian population.

However, in the absence of effective and accountable governance structures and systems to manage these stockpiles, many of the weapons collected – along with thousands of other officially procured SALW – continue to find their way into the hands of the DRC's many non-state armed groups. Safeguards to prevent weapons leakage from state stockpiles represent a critical linkage between SSR and SALW programming that has not been developed.

The failure of SSR programming to tackle widespread corruption in the DRC's security institutions has undercut SALW reduction and control initiatives. Resolving to pay soldiers an adequate wage and undertake a comprehensive anti-corruption campaign within the FARDC, all under the auspices of the SSR agenda, would likely improve the long-term prospects of SALW and DDR programming. Fighting corruption in the security sector remains a critical challenge to managing and safeguarding government weapons stockpiles.

Border management, another a priority area for SSR–SALW integration, has received scant attention in the DRC. Measures put in place to stop rampant illicit weapons trafficking at the borders – a major driver of conflict in the country and region – have been inadequate. Even under an international arms embargo since 2003, illicit weapons have flowed freely across the DRC's borders.

SSR programming has been unable to create either public trust in the security forces or a basic level of citizen security, both of which are key enabling conditions for SALW programming. In fact, the predatory nature of the country's security forces in spite of reform efforts has been a major deterrent to individual, community and group participation in SALW reduction and initiatives. As long as civilians feel they need arms for self-protection, including from the security forces themselves, the trafficking and widespread illicit possession of SALW will persist. There is no shortage of regional conventions and guidance to support constructive integrated action on SSR and SALW issues in the DRC, but this has not yet translated into tangible progress on the ground.

The DRC represents a failure of SSR–SALW integration, an outcome determined partially by the onerous conditions on the ground, where active conflict continues in parts of the country. However, despite the ongoing conflict, progress was made at different junctures to collect weapons in locally driven and internationally supported DDR and SALW reduction and control projects. It was the failure to launch effective complementary reforms of the security sector to consolidate the gains made by those initiatives that undermined wider reform progress. Even in very difficult contexts for SSR, as the Afghan case also shows, limited progress can be made to advance SSR and SALW programming goals if they are approached in a joined-up fashion.

Afghanistan

The Afghan government's 2005 Millennium Development Goals report explicitly recognizes the inextricable link between SSR and SALW reduction and control initiatives and the importance of both in advancing security and stability. However, it tends to view SALW programming as a distant or ancillary goal to be achieved only after meaningful reforms have been enacted in the security sector. The report argues, "Large-scale civilian disarmament, without the strengthening and reform of the police and justice systems, is likely to be both difficult and may also increase peoples' vulnerability and perception of mistrust of the state." It goes on to state that "the registration and regulation of small arms may be a more viable option" when reforms in the security sector have reached a more advanced stage.[368] The report seemingly ignores the reciprocal importance of SALW reduction and control in facilitating SSR, an omission clearly perceptible in the approach taken by the Afghan government and international donor community towards the SSR and demilitarization processes.

The implementation of the SSR process in Afghanistan has been encumbered by the absence of parallel steps to address the issue of SALW proliferation, a significant driver of insecurity. It is the persistence and gradual expansion of insecurity, in the form of a Taliban-led insurgency, warlordism and general criminality – all fuelled by the widespread availability of SALW – that has stood as a profound obstacle to SSR and the broader peacebuilding and statebuilding projects. As Chivers explains, "Afghanistan today would be less dangerous for almost all involved – civilians, government officials, nongovernment organizations, journalists, Afghan military and police forces, and Western troops" if SALW "were not so widely present in the field", yet "there has never been a successful, comprehensive military small-arms disarmament program in the country; instead, more guns keep flowing in".[369] The SSR model is ill suited to succeed in contexts facing high levels of insecurity and political instability. Accordingly, initiatives to control and collect the principal instrument of violence in the Afghan context, SALW, will help to mitigate such conditions and facilitate reform.

SSR, DDR and SALW programming

In Afghanistan DDR must be understood within a broader framework of demilitarization. Several interlinked initiatives have been undertaken under the auspices of demilitarization, including a DDR programme focused on the assemblage of militias that constituted the Northern Alliance, dubbed the Afghan Military Force (AMF); the Disbandment of Illegal Armed Groups (DIAG) programme that targeted all armed groups in the country outside the AMF, which are deemed illegal; the Heavy Weapons Cantonment Programme that sought to collect, deactivate and canton heavy weapons in the hands of non-state actors; and an ammunition and mine action programme mandated to collect, stockpile and destroy the estimated 100,000 tonnes of uncontrolled ammunition and explosive material littering the country.[370]

The key implementing body for demilitarization programming was the Afghanistan New Beginnings Programme (ANBP), which was established through a partnership between UNDP and the UN Assistance Mission in Afghanistan. Although Japan was recognized as the lead donor for demilitarization activities and the Afghan government was intended to be the key policymaking actor through its Demobilization and Reintegration Commission, the UN drove the process from its inception. But while the UN played a key role in the elaboration of the DDR process, its involvement in SSR has always been limited.[371]

The Afghan DDR process, which ran from 2003 to 2006, was one of the largest in history. The stated goal of the process was:

> To decommission formations and units up to a total of 100,000 officers and soldiers and in the process to collect, store and deactivate weapons currently in their possession in order to be able to reconstruct the Afghan National Army (ANA) and return those not required to civilian life.[372]

While disarmament was identified as a central goal of DDR, in practice it was treated as a peripheral aspect. The two underlying objectives of the process were "to break the historic patriarchical [*sic*] chain of command existing between the former commanders and their men; and to provide the demobilized personnel with the ability to become economically independent".[373] The disarmament and demobilization phase of the DDR process formally came to an end on 7 July 2005. It saw the demobilization of 63,380 ex-combatants and the collection of 57,629 SALW.[374] Despite these accomplishments, the patronage-based networks that sustained Afghanistan's local militias survived the DDR programme intact in most areas; security conditions have steadily deteriorated since the conclusion of the programme in 2006; and public faith in the state's ability to secure and safeguard the population has wavered.[375]

Progress in SSR has been uneven across its various pillars. Modest gains made in training and equipping the ANA belie the poor progress made in police, judicial and corrections reforms.[376] Moreover, key areas of the SSR agenda, such as the development of executive and legislative oversight mechanisms, the application of sound public finance management procedures and the empowerment of civil society, have received scant attention. This, in a sense, can be understood as a natural feature of an SSR process "under fire", a process being implemented during a conflict rather than in a post-conflict environment, and in a situation where non-state armed groups are increasing in strength rather than being disbanded and disarmed.[377]

As stated, the Afghan SSR and demilitarization processes largely advanced along two parallel tracks. Although DDR was framed as a pillar of the SSR process, it was designed and implemented as a stand-alone programme. As one senior ANBP official stated in 2009, "DDR was in isolation ... [and] lacked official connectivity with the other four SSR pillars".[378] Surprisingly little thinking was dedicated to the integration of SSR and DDR programming. Collaboration between the SSR process and demilitarization programming increased somewhat under the auspices of the DIAG programme, the successor initiative to DDR. In 2008 the government authorized the creation of a central DIAG unit in the Ministry of Interior. The unit comprised three sections: operations, PSC registration and individual weapons registration.[379] Its establishment was intended to foster greater integration of police development and SALW reduction and control activities. When the DIAG programme came to an end in March 2011 it had disbanded 759 armed groups – just more than half of the 1,496 illegal armed groups it had targeted – collecting 54,138 weapons, a fraction of those believed to be circulating.[380] Few attempts have been made to address the remaining illegally armed groups and their weapons holdings, and there were signs in late 2012 and early 2013 that the trade in illegal weapons in Afghanistan had heated up, with individual Afghans and groups stocking up on guns in advance of the drawdown of NATO's military mission in the country.[381] This trend saw no sign of abating following the withdrawal of the bulk of NATO forces in 2014, with the overall security situation experiencing a marked deterioration.[382]

On the issue of SALW stockpile management and procurement in the Afghan security sector, the United States supported the strengthening of the Department for Acquisitions, Technology and Logistics (AT&L) within the Ministry of Defence, one of whose functions was to oversee procurement of SALW. Despite investments in developing procurement systems, the AT&L has consistently performed poorly in fulfilling one of its primary functions: assuring end-user accountability of all distributed weapons.[383]

A July 2014 report by the US Special Inspector General for Afghanistan Reconstruction painted an alarming picture of ANA mismanagement of weapons donated by the United States and other NATO partners. Of the 474,823 weapons, primarily SALW,[384] provided by the US Department of Defense to the ANA since 2004, 43 per cent (203,888 weapons) could not be accounted for.[385] The report concluded that there was a "real potential for these weapons to fall into the hands of insurgents, which will pose additional risks to U.S. personnel, the ANSF [Afghan National Security Forces], and Afghan civilians".[386] In fact, there have been numerous reports dating back to the early days of the SSR process that donated weapons were being sold to the Taliban and other anti-government armed groups.[387]

It is important to note that individual members of the Afghan National Police tend to treat their duty weapons as personal possessions, reinforcing the police's lack of accountability to the state and perpetuating a culture of impunity. Indeed, this is true of all equipment provided to the police in the context of the reform process.[388] For instance, one police chief dismissed by the government in 2005 had pilfered all the new equipment provided to his unit through the reform process, including office furniture, vehicles, communications equipment and firearms.[389] There are also many examples of weapons leakage from the Ministry of Interior, with duty weapons appearing on the black market or in the arsenals of anti-government armed groups.[390]

The existence of large numbers of non-statutory or informal security actors in Afghanistan has acted as a driver of weapons proliferation. These groups are varied, ranging from semi-formal actors such as PSCs and militias operating under the umbrella of the formal security sector to illegal groupings such as insurgent militias. They have fuelled the illicit market in SALW and facilitated internal and cross-border arms flows.[391] Attempts to regulate semi-formal armed actors and contain their illegal counterparts have been ineffectual.[392]

Beyond the regular police units – the Afghan Uniformed Police, Afghan Civil Order Police (responsible for special operations) and Afghan Border Police – the Ministry of Interior commands an irregular police force, the Afghan Local Police (ALP). Numbering 30,000 in late 2015, the ALP comprises groups of locally recruited militiamen provided with rudimentary training by US Special Forces.[393] Formed in 2010 under the authority of the Ministry of Interior, the ALP has been the subject of significant criticism inside and outside Afghanistan due to the perception that it provides an umbrella of legitimacy for illegal armed groups and "its short-term gains in territory will come at the expense of future stability, as armed groups proliferate outside of the state's control".[394] The ALP follows in the footsteps of a number of failed initiatives to mobilize informal security actors at the local level to fill security gaps, such as the Afghan Guard Force and the Afghan National Auxiliary Police. The Ministry of Interior has stressed that the ALP is a temporary structure and will be scaled back and integrated into the uniformed police by 2018, although few concrete details have been divulged on how this will be accomplished.[395]

While the notion of exploiting informal and traditional security structures to fill the prevailing security vacuum is surely compelling, it has the potential to exacerbate insecurity, undercut the demilitarization project and drive SALW proliferation. Accordingly, the use of militias to complement and support the ANSF has been met with opposition by large sections of the international community and members of the government.[396]

It is important to note that demilitarization activities have overlapped with the judicial and legal reform process in the development of laws governing weapon ownership and possession. However, even in this area the judicial and demilitarization spheres have tended to act in parallel rather than in concert. After the fall of the Taliban regime, Afghanistan's laws regulating firearm possession were convoluted, poorly understood and rarely enforced. Consistent with the wider judicial reform process, efforts to rationalize legal statutes regarding SALW were characterized by inertia during the first two years of the reconstruction process. Despite the importance of endowing the demilitarization process with a solid legal foundation, little consideration was accorded to reforms of the existing weapons laws until 2004, when President Karzai issued an important presidential decree that endowed the demilitarization process with the political authority it required. The decree, issued on 14 July 2004, recognized disarmament as "one of the substantial conditions of the restoration of law, provision of a permanent peace, improvement of the economic situation, safeguarding of human rights and ruling on the basis of people's will".[397] The decree went on to threaten "the severest punishment for any actors who attempted to circumvent the process and maintain armed groups".[398] It paved the way for a new law on SALW.

The Law on Fire Weapons, Ammunitions and Explosive Materials, which came into force on 24 June 2005, gave the demilitarization process the legal basis it was lacking. It firmly establishes that "the government has sovereignty over those fire weapons, ammunitions and explosive materials which are existing in this country" and affirms that "other persons and authorities without legal permission have no right to produce, import, export, gain, use and keep them".[399] The law outlines a licensing and registration system for the acquisition, possession and sale of SALW, to be managed and overseen by the Ministry of Interior. It stipulates that a weapons licence must feature a photo of the licensee and list the weapon's serial number. Failure to register a weapon will result in fines commensurate to the value of the weapon and associated ammunition, confiscation and legal prosecution.

In its first four years of operation the number of privately owned weapons registered by the state under the law was negligible (roughly 15,000).[400] This can be attributed to both a lack of capacity to carry out registration and the adverse security climate. As the 2005 Millennium Development Goals country report states, "encouraging those who currently own weapons to apply for licenses, and identifying and punishing those who fail to comply with the new law will be a resource-intensive process".[401] The Afghan National Police lacked the means to carry out basic policing functions, thus the enforcement of a countrywide registration system remained beyond its capability.

Another legal statute that seeks to regulate gun ownership focuses on the private security industry. After 2001 the number of PSCs, primarily international, operating in Afghanistan rose exponentially. PSCs both surreptitiously imported weapons, circumventing Afghan customs duties and import regulations, and illegally purchased arms on the black market.[402] In 2005 the government developed legislation that would curb such actions through the establishment of a comprehensive registration system. The Law on Private Security Organizations requires PSCs, individual contractors and any associated armed personnel to acquire permits to operate and carry firearms. Annual fees are levied for registration,[403] with contractors required to submit fingerprints, photographs and detailed personal information upon application for a licence.[404] Despite the promulgation of these laws, very few transgressors have been tried in the Afghan courts. There is insufficient capacity or will on the part of the Afghan Attorney General's Office to prosecute weapons cases.[405]

Lessons learned

The widespread availability of SALW in Afghanistan poses a salient risk to the country. Beyond the obvious public safety and health risks that SALW present, they have facilitated the growth of the illicit economy – typified by the drug trade – and an unrelenting anti-government insurgency. Warlords have used their weapons to carve out spheres of influence, assuring their autonomy and preventing the government from extending its writ across the country.

The demilitarization of society, the establishment of a legal framework to control arms proliferation and the formation of a coherent policy on weapons stockpile management and procurement represent the three points of what can be conceptualized as a SALW triad in Afghanistan. Addressing the problem of SALW proliferation here and in other FFCAS requires parallel progress at each of these points – something that has not occurred in the Afghan context, where very little attention has been accorded to the SALW issue despite the massive scale of arms possession and trafficking. Disarmament was only a symbolic element of the DDR process; little consideration was given to the legal dimension of the issue until 2005 and a rational procurement policy for the security forces was slow to develop.

This limited progress made in addressing the SALW problem can partially be attributed to conditions that were inhospitable for action on the issue. The Afghan case aptly illustrates that the potential for SALW reduction and control programming is dependent on the presence of a number of conditions, notably a stable and secure environment, development opportunities and robust political will. The failure of the government to develop and reform the security sector, particularly the police, in such a manner as to foster public trust in its ability to provide a basic level of public security has hampered efforts to address the rampant problem of SALW proliferation. Linkages between SALW reduction and control efforts and the SSR agenda were never clearly established, with cooperation tending to be *ad hoc* rather than institutionalized. This missed vital entry points to bolster both processes and contribute to the broader stabilization of the country. Despite the investment of high levels of resources, in terms of both technical capacity and funds, into SSR, SALW and DDR programming in Afghanistan, their cumulative achievements have been limited. While the difficult ground-level security and political conditions represent the most prominent factor inhibiting progress, it can also be attributed to the failure to develop integrated implementation structures and strategies. There were major disconnects in donor approaches to SSR, SALW and DDR programming, which also suffered from poor levels of local ownership. The Afghan case exemplifies how even extensive human and material resources, in this case provided by external donors, cannot compensate for poorly integrated programming.

Comparing and contrasting the case studies

The case studies offer a menu of different configurations of the SSR–SALW relationship in FFCAS. An assessment of the ground-level impacts achieved by SSR and SALW programming in each case provides a strong argument for their integration in policy and practice. The Albanian, Cambodian and El Salvadorian cases represent partial success stories of SSR–SALW integration, although following different paths to joined-up programming. In Albania and Cambodia it was robust SALW reduction and control programming early in the transition period that created entry points for SSR initiatives to take shape. In both cases, locally owned SALW collection and destruction initiatives carved out space for vital reforms of the security sector. Significant integration of SSR and SALW programming was a notable feature of the Albanian and Cambodian cases, but disconnects evolved over time that hampered progress for both. For instance, in Cambodia a holistic, governance-focused SSR programme never emerged, obstructing efforts to consolidate a long-term weapons control regime.

El Salvador demonstrated both the benefits of integration and the deleterious implications of disconnected SSR and SALW programming. During the first decade after the 1992 peace accord with the FMLN gains were made in both SSR and DDR, due in large part to significant levels of integration of the two projects. However, once the DDR programme came to an end the focus shifted almost entirely to SSR, ignoring the SALW dilemma despite the widespread circulation of illicit arms. The upsurge in organized crime that the pervasive availability of SALW facilitated gradually triggered backsliding on SSR, bringing to the fore old tensions and anxieties over the militarization of policing and politics that drove previous conflict dynamics. There was very little political will to advance SALW programming, which subsequently undermined SSR.

The Malawi case is an exemplar of SSR–SALW integration. SALW reduction and control programming advanced relatively seamlessly with the development of a robust community policing model that helped to forge the indispensible public trust for SSR and SALW programme implementation. These initiatives were locally owned with targeted technical support from donors, and featured a holistic approach in line with SSR orthodoxy. The programmes did not just seek to train new police and collect weapons, but to improve governance in the security sector and establish sound regulatory systems for SALW control. All this was achieved with limited resources, although in a political and security environment far more permissive and secure than the failed cases of the DRC and Afghanistan.

In many ways the DRC and Afghan cases show the limitations of advancing SSR and SALW programming, whether integrated or stand-alone, in conflict-affected environments where a clear political settlement is lacking. Both cases feature SSR and SALW initiatives that were advanced in parallel, but with only marginal and largely superficial mutual engagement. The DRC features a range of different SALW reduction and control initiatives championed by different actors with marginal connections to broader SSR processes. In Afghanistan the multiplicity of different actors, both internal and external, operating in the SSR, SALW and DDR spheres, many with conflicting visions and objectives, made integration of programming almost impossible. In fact, SSR programming in some instances directly counteracted ongoing demilitarization activities. In both cases SSR and SALW programmes were largely externally driven, with little local political will to move them forward. Accordingly, the impacts they achieved were disappointing.

Despite the adverse conditions that prevailed in the DRC and Afghanistan, the poor record of SSR and SALW programming reinforces the importance of SSR–SALW integration in FFCAS. The difficult conditions actually made integration even more vital to take advantage of narrow windows of opportunity and exploit often limited political will. Given that public trust in the security sectors of both countries is particularly precarious, it is difficult to envision gains made in SALW reduction and control without associated improvements in the quality and professionalism of the security forces, and vice versa.

This paper is by no means arguing that joined-up SSR and SALW programmes alone can guarantee positive impacts for SSR and SALW programming in FFCAS, or overcome the many challenges facing broader peacebuilding programmes. Indeed, the successful and partially successful cases discussed here feature a range of favourable conditions and variables not present in the failed cases. Instead, the paper argues that the level of integration of these programmes is one factor that can improve their efficacy in complex FFCAS contexts.

The survey of the case studies zeroed in on a number of specific thematic and programmatic areas that should serve as priority focal points of enhanced SSR–SALW integration. The first, the security dilemma, is an overarching, cross-cutting issue that frames both the challenge and the imperative of integration; it should dictate the form programmatic integration should take on the ground. The other three – stockpile management and weapons procurement, border control and legal instruments for weapons control and oversight – mirror the practical areas of convergence laid out earlier. While DDR represents, as already detailed, a well-established point of SSR–SALW programmatic convergence, this section focuses on the areas where SSR–SALW linkages are most underdeveloped and the need for integration and the potential to achieve it are most robust. Although DDR programmes in many contexts should be more explicitly designed and operated to draw SSR and SALW programming closer together, they already establish strong conceptual and technical links between the two. It is also important to note that stockpile management and weapons procurement are approached together in the following analysis to reflect the manner in which they were characteristically treated in the case studies, as two sides of the same coin.

The security dilemma

It is the security dilemma experienced by communities in almost all conflict-affected environments that ties SSR and SALW programmes together. General populations, armed groups and even the state invariably feel varying levels of anxiety over security conditions in the aftermath of conflicts, due to either residual political violence or a rise in criminality. When it comes to non-state actors and communities, this anxiety tends to manifest itself as a lack of confidence in the state's ability to provide security and access to justice in a fair and transparent fashion. The anxiety is more pronounced when the state security forces were a party to the previous conflict or implicated in atrocities and other human rights violations against the civilian population. All the case studies, to varying degrees, show that a lack of trust in the security forces, most often the police, was a decisive incentive for civilians to retain and acquire weapons for self-defence. In the case of the DRC, the FARDC was clearly viewed by large swathes of the population as a source of predation rather than protection, particularly in the conflict-affected eastern region of the country. The case studies make it abundantly clear that without fundamental reforms in the security sector that can better prepare security institutions to meet the security needs of the population, SALW programmes will be unviable. The UN's IDDRS recognizes this fact, explaining that both civilian disarmament and DDR processes "should be based on a level of confidence that can be fostered through broader SSR measures (such as police or corrections reform)" which can contribute to "an increased level of community security and provide the necessary reassurance that these weapons are no longer necessary".[406] It would, in the words of Ebo, "demonstrate to the citizens that self-help security measures are no longer necessary".[407]

The failure to address the proliferation of SALW in FFCAS also contributes to insecurity and can obstruct genuine attempts to transform the security sector. In El Salvador positive headway on SSR early in the post-conflict period was gradually undermined by a failure to address SALW proliferation. The wide availability of SALW helped to facilitate the rise of organized crime and armed violence that overwhelmed the country's police. This trend reversed many of the impressive gains made in the Salvadorian SSR process, most worryingly leading to the remilitarization of some policing functions. As the case studies show, joined-up SSR–SALW activity will help to address the fundamental security dilemma that challenges the implementation of both programmes.

Stockpile management and weapons procurement
Corruption within the security sector is a driver not only of dysfunction within the state but also of weapons proliferation throughout the country. Procurement practices and weapons stockpile management systems are always epicentres of corruption in FFCAS. This typically takes the form of weapons leakage to non-state armed groups. In the DRC poor stockpile management, a culture of impunity, endemic corruption and low or nonexistent oversight of the security forces have led to the widespread diversion of government weapons stocks. The problem of corruption as it pertains to SALW is not confined to the macro state level, but is present at the micro level in how individual security forces and community-level security personnel perceive and handle their weapons. In Afghanistan individual policemen typically view their duty weapons as personal possessions and have been prone either to sell these weapons or employ them for personal gain, such as participating in criminal activities. Addressing the associated issues of corruption and stockpile management in the security sector requires joint action by SSR and SALW programmes. However, too often these areas receive limited attention. Civilian populations and non-state armed groups alike will understandably resist participation in state-run or state-supported disarmament programmes if they lack confidence that the state can safely secure and store the weapons submitted. The establishment of effective and accountable stockpile management systems is a key objective of SSR programming that is also vital for the efficacy of SALW initiatives.

Border control
All the cases analysed for this study can be seen as part of regional conflict formations or zones of instability. Conflict dynamics are not confined to their national territories. Drivers of instability, including the supply of weapons, have emanated from beyond their borders. Moreover, instability and conflict in each of these countries have contributed to regional and global weapons proliferation. Afghanistan,

for instance, has been a destination for weapons and fighters from its neighbours and global superpowers alike for decades, while the crisis in Albania helped to fuel weapons trafficking across the Balkans and Western Europe. The regional nature of conflicts and crises in most FFCAS, including those examined in this study, demands particular types of joint interventions from SSR and SALW programmers. One such joint intervention is to expand the capacity of border and customs management agencies to contain illicit cross-border weapons trafficking. However, they can also take the form of broader regional weapons management programmes and embargos. Several regional regulatory regimes, outlined at the beginning of the paper, seek to establish common standards for weapons control and facilitate the sharing of information and best practices across states, but they have not led to the formation of substantive and concrete regional SALW reduction and control initiatives. The areas of border enforcement and regional regulatory structures both received insufficient attention in the case studies analysed for this paper. They represent a critical area of overlap between SSR and SALW programming where increased investment could make significant headway.

Legal instruments for weapons control and oversight
Across the case studies, the design and reform of weapons laws and statutes represent a critical step of SALW programming. However, while this lays an important foundation for SALW reduction and control activities, it tends not to be accompanied by the creation of infrastructure for implementation, which falls under the remit of SSR. In addition to the training of security forces, this would involve the development of governance mechanisms like licensing schemes, weapons databases and marking systems typically managed by police services and interior ministries. Whether because of absent political will, poor design or shortfalls in resources and capacity, weapons laws have remained paper tigers in many cases. They may be well designed, but are rarely applied in a comprehensive manner due in part to insufficient investment in implementing structures under the auspices of SSR programmes. Establishing robust regulatory regimes for SALW, with the appropriate institutional machinery and human capacity to manage them, represents a critical area for long-term collaboration between security sector reformers and SALW practitioners.

The case studies show that SSR and SALW projects and programmes can indeed be mutually reinforcing or detrimental, depending on their orientation and level of integration. Taken together, the analysis of the case studies makes a strong case to advance SSR and SALW in a joined-up fashion.

Conclusion

A notable lesson of the experience in stabilizing and reconstructing FFCAS over the past decade is that SSR and the reduction and control of SALW are intricately connected. The failure to recognize the symbiotic relationship between them could in turn do harm to the wider goals of the peacebuilding and statebuilding projects of which they are parts. Investing the state with a monopoly over the use of coercive force in a manner consistent with good governance principles and democratic norms – the primary goal of SSR – is dependent to a certain degree on the removal of weapons and the breakdown of militant groups that can fuel political and criminal violence. Inversely, non-state armed groups and communities alike will invariably resist SALW reduction and control programmes unless they feel the state is capable of providing a base level of security and justice in an effective and equitable manner. As such, SSR and SALW efforts are interdependent and will benefit from more intensive coordination and integration.

With the SSR model now under intense scrutiny from policymakers, practitioners and analysts due to its mixed record of achievement, the ground is fertile for conceptual change. The prevailing critiques of SSR are related to wider critical discourse surrounding peacebuilding and statebuilding orthodoxy that has opened the door for new ideas and approaches. Integrating SSR and SALW policy and practice at the international policy level as well as in implementation settings represents a modest shift in approach that could deliver significant dividends.

However, achieving this shift will require a political commitment to challenging entrenched interests and rigid practices that have proven resistant to change. This would, as Bourne and Greene suggest, require "substantial 're-packing' and integration of DDR, SSR and SALW control elements ... and greater international capacity and will to develop, implement and support context-specific security-building or armed violence reduction strategies over a sustained period".[408]

Beyond limiting progress in statebuilding and peacebuilding projects, the failure to exploit synergies between SSR and SALW programming can actually stoke instability. Ineffective, repressive or corrupt security sectors can increase demand for militias and weapons, and, conversely, the proliferation of armed individuals and groups can lead to the breakdown of state order and the militarization of security structures.

While there is broad agreement that SSR and SALW programmes are intertwined, there are few examples where they have been comprehensively planned, designed, implemented and evaluated in an integrated fashion. This has perhaps contributed to the mixed record of achievement of SSR and SALW programming in FFCAS. Analysis of the SSR–SALW relationship in implementation settings reveals a significant gap between policy and practice. The following recommendations provide some steps to narrow this gap. They are not necessarily novel, often reflecting existing guidance in conceptual and policy documents on SSR and SALW, but they are rarely translated into programmatic action. If anything, this paper represents a call to heed the lessons and insights already learned in the field and design and implement programmes accordingly.

Introduce a unified political approach

A lack of political will to advance SSR and SALW individually, let alone as a joint project, presents one of the preeminent challenges to both. For instance, shortfalls of political will to advance SALW reduction and control programming in tandem with SSR in El Salvador enabled the proliferation of weapons and organized crime, which subsequently led to reform reversals in the security sector. In the DRC the absence of political consensus in support of SSR and disarmament efforts meant that most initiatives were small and *ad hoc*, with limited impact. By contrast, the strong base of political support underlying holistic SALW and SSR programming in Malawi – comprising government, civil society and a small cadre of donors – gave it a durable foundation to succeed in spite of limited resources.

SSR and SALW programmes invariably involve the reshaping of power dynamics and the transformation of the political and institutional landscape of the security sector, thus they often encounter serious spoiler activity from both mainstream and fringe actors alike. Building a political consensus around SSR and SALW action that emphasizes the utility of programmatic integration is critical. Achieving this type of consensus requires external donors and domestic champions of reform to expend significant political capital, which they have generally been reticent to do.

Develop joint technical and coordination capacity
Integrating SSR and SALW involves above all else the merging of institutional machinery and human capacity that has developed over the past decade in key international and bilateral stakeholders. Separate units addressing SSR and SALW should either be better coordinated or merged outright. Planning and strategy documents should be jointly developed, and missions in the field should combine SSR and SALW expertise. Separate institutional structures as well as stand-alone policy and implementation models can obstruct innate synergies and opportunities for joint action. We saw this in Afghanistan, where donor programmes supporting SSR and demilitarization activities were advanced in silos with little mutual understanding, let alone concrete collaboration. As a result, few programmatic linkages were developed despite natural synergies and clear entry points for joint action. The failure to leverage scarce resources and political opportunities through integration set back both processes.

The resources invested in SSR and SALW activities in FFCAS could be pooled to facilitate better integration. This does not obviate the need for specialized expertise in specific areas of SSR and SALW programming, but rather highlights the need for greater overarching unity of thought and practice in how the two projects are approached at both the headquarters and field levels.

Establish joint, field-level governance arrangements
In the field, SSR and SALW programmes should be combined under joint governance arrangements that ensure collaboration in a number of key areas throughout the life cycle of both programmes. These include information sharing, assessments, monitoring and evaluation, programme design, resource management and messaging and communications. Ensuring that SALW and SSR programmes are advanced under the auspices of common management structures will ensure that opportunities for resource sharing, joint messaging and unified crisis response are not missed. Most importantly, it will ensure that each project contributes to creating conditions for mutual success.

So often, SALW and SSR programmes are advanced sequentially rather than concurrently, which misses opportunities for resource sharing. When it come to the relationship between SSR and DDR, the OECD-DAC *Handbook* acknowledges that "it is often assumed that SSR will follow a DDR programme, but decisions on the appropriate levels of security forces and the number and type of ex-combatants to be integrated into them should be taken prior to demobilisation".[409] In other words, the two programmes need to be aligned from the very outset, not in a staggered fashion as particular milestones are achieved. The handbook goes on to recommend that SSR and DDR "issues are often best considered together as part of a comprehensive security and justice development programme".[410]This logic, which also applies to the SSR–SALW relationship, is characteristically not actualized in programming. For instance, in the DRC conventional wisdom dictated that comprehensive SSR should take place only after DDR programmes had completed the bulk of their work. An outlier, as reflected in this paper, is the Malawi case, which featured a joined-up approach that unified SALW and SSR activities under a single umbrella. This facilitated the leveraging of scarce resources and political will across programmatic boundaries and exemplified the advantages of developing joint governance arrangements for SSR and SALW programming.

Implement existing agreements and protocols

As the opening section of this paper demonstrates, there are numerous international agreements and protocols that provide guidance for every facet of the SALW issue, from the regulation of the licit SALW trade to the collection and destruction of surplus SALW. These agreements also call for robust collaboration with SSR programming as a prerequisite for success. Implementation of such agreements and protocols at the national level in FFCAS has lagged, due in part to the absence of concrete regional and multilateral institutional structures that can directly assist SALW programming and encourage concrete links with national-level SSR agendas. For instance, despite being a signatory to the Nairobi Protocol, the government of the DRC did not, as of 2015, have proper safeguards to prevent the leakage of legal weapons and ammunition. Even the most expertly crafted legal frameworks and protocols will be hard pressed to compensate for major implementation capacity deficits, as seen in the DRC.

In light of the regional and international nature of the SALW proliferation problem, establishing supranational instruments with direct programming capacity to assist practically in implementation could bear significant fruit.

However, concerns over national sovereignty and resource constraints have confined these matters to the purview of national governments, whose responses have been inconsistent and insufficient. Establishing institutional arrangements with greater teeth in regional bodies such as the AU to facilitate the application of existing protocols, with an emphasis on provisions to strengthen linkages with SSR activity, could provide a vital boost to national-level SSR and SALW programmes.

Focus on procurement and anti-corruption

As the case studies show, weapons procurement is a flashpoint for mismanagement and dysfunction in FFCAS, which can have the dual effect of funnelling arms into the illicit weapons trade and fostering corruption within the state that can undermine the legitimacy and integrity of the security establishment. The widespread leakage of government weapons and ammunition stocks in the DRC and Afghanistan, a major driver of criminal and political violence, exemplifies the importance of establishing robust procurement and weapons management systems. In these cases, flawed procurement systems intended to facilitate the equipping of the reforming security forces did significant harm.

There are significant gaps in the existing SSR guidance literature on how to support the development of such regulatory systems. Effort should be made to develop guidance and best practices surrounding procurement capacity building in FFCAS. Donors should invest in creating standing international capacity that can be rapidly deployed to assist FFCAS to undertake these reforms. A natural area of overlap between SSR and SALW activity, capacity building in SALW procurement systems in the security sector represents an important target area for increased investment.

Include SALW in police training and reform programmes

The police is the most prominent security sector actor involved in SALW reduction and control activities. It is for this reason that the IDDRS recommends that "disarmament programmes should be complemented, where appropriate, by training and other activities to enhance law enforcement capacities and national control over weapons and ammunition stocks".[411] Most training curricula developed under the auspices of police reform programmes in FFCAS include instruction on various topics touching on SALW, from duty weapon management to advanced forensics and ballistics. The JSAC programme in Cambodia, as an example, funded seminars to educate the police, military and other security sector actors on the country's Law on Weapons, Explosives and Ammunition Management. It is important that every training and capacity-building programme includes a robust module on SALW reduction and control that will cover a range of topics, from managing official stockpiles to weapons collection practices. Developing a standard curriculum module, adaptable to different environments, that can be integrated into police training programmes would help to solidify the link between SSR and SALW work in a sustainable manner.

Prioritize awareness raising

An area of SSR programming that is characteristically neglected is public information and education activities. In the midst of a security transition it is critical to sensitize publics about the goals of SSR and the role of citizens within the changing security sector, and to contain unrealistic expectations regarding the pace of the reform process and its immediate public dividends. SALW reduction and control programmes have a significantly better record than SSR programmes in utilizing public awareness campaigns to advance their goals. The SALW reduction and control programmes in Albania, Cambodia and Malawi discussed in this paper included strong awareness-raising components. All these in turn featured healthy levels of community and civil society engagement.

It could be advantageous to develop common public information campaigns that address SSR and SALW not as stand-alone issues but as a part of an integrated agenda. This would help the general public to understand better the role of the state in advancing public security and imbue the national government with clearer ownership of the process. In light of how perceptions of insecurity and the state's ability to provide protection shape public attitudes towards SSR and SALW activities, such joint messaging can play a crucial role in advancing both processes. Joint awareness-raising activities enable the maximization of scarce resources and can foster the vital public trust required for success.

Integrate SALW into SSR assessments and planning

An important mechanism to ensure the appropriate integration of SSR and SALW reduction and control activities is to conduct joint assessments, programme planning and monitoring and evaluation activities throughout the life cycles of both programmes. Crucially, SALW specialists should be engaged in the initial assessment that informs SSR strategy design. SALW issues should also factor into any threat and conflict analysis that informs the development of the SSR agenda. Indeed, the IDDRS recommends that "SALW availability should be a component of conflict and security analysis" that forms the bedrock of SSR programme planning.[412] Strong programmatic linkages should be developed among SALW and SSR initiatives, buttressed and facilitated by cross-appointed expertise. The success of the Malawian SALW and SSR programmes stems from the fact that they were integrated at all stages of the programming cycle, from inception to completion. Such an approach could enhance the efficacy of SALW and SSR programming in other FFCAS.

More donor accountability

External bilateral donors play a vital role in supporting SSR and SALW programmes in FFCAS. As a part of this assistance they often supply weapons to endow the partner security sector with the capacity to establish a monopoly of coercive force, and in some cases to advance donor strategic priorities. In cases like Afghanistan there are scores of examples of donor-supplied weapons that were misappropriated or leaked to non-state armed groups. There is a tendency among donors to attribute such governance breakdowns to dysfunction in recipient states. However, such weapons diversions are as much a result of weak donor verification systems, whose purpose is to confirm that weapons deliveries have reached the correct recipient. Greater responsibility must be assumed by donors to ensure that monitoring systems for supplied arms are functional, robust and coordinated with the recipient country's procurement and stockpile management systems. The imperative of establishing effective monitoring and verification systems for supplied weapons and equipment must be factored into SSR planning and implementation. Decision-making on the type of equipment to be provided to recipient countries as part of SSR programmes must carefully consider the capabilities of donors and recipients to verify the end use of that equipment.

Adopt a long-term focus

The bulk of the focus on SALW issues in FFCAS comes in the immediate aftermath of a conflict, when the country is rife with weapons, conflict fatigue is high and political will for change is strong, both domestically and among external donors. There is a window of opportunity for SALW reduction and control in the aftermath of a conflict, but it is critical to remember that "disarmament is not just a short-term security measure designed to collect surplus weapons and ammunition. It is also implicitly part of a broader process of state regulation and control over the transfer, trafficking and use of weapons within a national territory."[413] Just as SSR is a generational project, so too is SALW control in the aftermath of state failure or conflict. It is important that all stakeholders in the process recognize the short-, medium- and long-term dimensions of both SSR and SALW programmes from the earliest phases of the projects and synchronize them accordingly. We have rarely seen this in practice, as the case studies in this paper demonstrate. Whether it is post-conflict states like El Salvador and Cambodia or countries with ongoing conflicts such as the DRC and Afghanistan, short-termism tends to be the order of the day, to the detriment of long-term stabilization and peace consolidation. The problem is that short-term programming consistently produces suboptimal and unsustainable outcomes. Until a shift in mind-set is achieved in how donors approach security transitions, assuming a long-term vision, overcoming many of the challenges outlined in this paper will be difficult.

With the SSR field entering a period of introspection, with many analysts, practitioners and policymakers discussing the necessity of systemic change, innovation and even a "second-generation" approach, the time is ripe to develop best practices for better integration of SSR and SALW programming in the field. The two projects are deeply interconnected in both conceptual and practical terms, with the case-study research illustrating that their outcomes are highly interdependent and mutually reinforcing. Another benefit of better programmatic integration is that it will enable more effective responses to emerging multi-dimensional security challenges, such as countering violent extremism and transnational organized crime, which require simultaneous SSR, SALW and DDR interventions. At the level of policy, there is already a wide awareness of the need to tie the two programme areas together. The difficult task now is to translate policy into practice.

Notes

1   United Nations, *Integrated Disarmament, Demobilization and Reintegration Standards: SALW Control, Security and Development*, Level 4.11 (New York: United Nations, 2006), p. 22.

2   Dominick Donald and Funmi Olonisakin, "Security sector reform and the demand for small arms and light weapons", Project Ploughshares Briefing 01-7, Waterloo, ON, 2001.

3   See Ernie Regehr, "Reducing the demand for small arms and light weapons: Priorities for the international community", Project Ploughshares Working Paper 04-02, Waterloo, ON, 2004; Kristiana Powell, "Security sector reform and the protection of civilians in Burundi: Accomplishments, dilemmas and ideas for international engagement", North-South Institute and Centre d'Alerte et de Prévention des Conflits working paper, Ottawa, ON, 2007, pp. 32–33.

4   United Nations, note 1 above, p. 22.

5   Ibid., p. 23.

6   Mark Sedra, "Transitioning from first to second generation security sector reform in conflict-affected countries", in Paul Jackson (ed.), *Handbook of International Security and Development* (Cheltenham: Edward Elgar Publishing, 2014).

7   OECD-DAC, *Handbook on Security System Reform: Supporting Security and Justice* (Paris: OECD, 2007), p. 106.

8   Ibid., p. 5.

9   Aaron Karp, "Man, the state, and war", in *Small Arms Survey 2009: Shadows of War* (Geneva: Cambridge University Press, 2009), p. 160.

10 Ibid.

11 Ibid., p. 161.

12 Clare Short, "Security sector reform and the elimination of poverty", speech at Centre for Defence Studies, King's College, London, March 1999.

13 Alex J. Bellamy, *"Security sector reform: Prospects and problems", Global Change, Peace & Security, 15(2), 2003, pp. 101–119 at p. 101.*

14 United Nations, *Security Sector Reform Integrated Technical Guidance Notes* (New York: United Nations, 2012), p. 5.

15 See, for instance, OECD-DAC, note 7 above; United Nations, "Securing peace and development: The role of the United Nations in supporting security sector reform", report of the Secretary-General, 23 January 2008, UN Doc. A/62/659-S/2008/39, www.securitycouncilreport.org/atf/cf/%7B65BFCF9B-6D27-4E9C-8CD3-CF6E4FF96FF9%7D/SSR%20S%202008%2039.pdf.

16 UN Development Programme, *Security Sector Reform and Transitional Justice: A Crisis Post-Conflict Programmatic Approach* (New York: UNDP, 2003), p. 5.

17 UN DPKO and UNMAS, "Security Council encourages UN representatives and envoys to consider the strategic value of security sector reform – Resolution 2151", 20 May 2014, www.un.int/news/security-council-encourages-un-representatives-and-envoys-consider-strategic-value-security.

18 Ibid.

19 Sedra, note 6 above.

20 UN Security Council, Resolution 2151, UN Doc. S/RES/2151 (2014), 28 April 2014.

21 Ibid.

22 UN DPKO and UNMAS, note 17 above.

23 Ibid.

24 Sedra, note 6 above.

25 OECD-DAC, note 7 above; United Nations, note 15 above.

26 Robert Egnell and Peter Haldén, "Laudable, ahistorical and overambitious: Security sector reform meets state formation theory", *Conflict, Security & Development,* 9(1), 2014, pp. 27–54 at p. 29.

27 Robert H. Jackson, *Quasi-States: Sovereignty, International Relations and the Third World* (Cambridge: Cambridge University Press, 1993).

28 OECD-DAC, note 7 above, p. 105.

29 Ibid., p. 105.

30 Sean McFate, "The link between DDR and SSR in conflict-affected countries", US Institute of Peace Special Report 238, USIP, Washington, DC, May 2010, p. 1.

31 UN Disarmament, Demobilization and Reintegration Resource Centre, "What is DDR?", May 2005, http://unddr.org/what-is-ddr/introduction_1.aspx.

32 Karp, note 9 above, p. 180.

33 Robert Muggah and Chris O'Donnell, "Next generation disarmament, demobilization and reintegration", *Stability: International Journal of Security and Development,* www.stabilityjournal.org/articles/10.5334/sta.fs/.

34 Ibid.

35 Ibid.

36 OECD-DAC, note 7 above, p. 106.

37 Ibid.

38 WHO, "Report of the World Health Organization", statement delivered to 2003 Conference to Review the UN Programme of Action on the Illicit Trade in Small Arms and Light Weapons.

39 Joakim Kreutz, Nicholas Marsh and Manuela Torre, "Regaining state control: Arms and violence in post-conflict countries", in Owen Greene and Nicholas Marsh (eds), *Small Arms, Crime and Conflict: Global Governance and the Threat of Armed Violence* (London: Routledge, 2012), p. 66.

40 Personal communication with senior UN official, 17 February 2016.

41 Mike Bourne and Owen Greene, "Governance and control of SALW after armed conflicts", in Owen Greene and Nicholas Marsh (eds), *Small Arms, Crime and Conflict: Global Governance and the Threat of Armed Violence* (London: Routledge, 2012), p. 188.

42 Ibid.

43 Personal communication with senior UN official, 17 February 2016.

44 Maria Stern and Joakim Öjendal, "Mapping the security-development nexus: Conflict, complexity, cacophony, convergence?", *Security Dialogue,* 41(1), 2010, pp. 5–29.

45 See Lisa Denney and Pilar Domingo, *Future Directions of Security and Justice: Context-Relevant, Flexible and Transitional Programming?* (London: Overseas Development Institute, 2015); Erwin van Veen, "Improving security and justice programming in fragile situations: Better political engagement, more change management", OECD Development Policy Papers No. 3, Paris, March 2016.

46 Personal communication with senior UN official, 17 February 2016.

47 Personal communication with Dean Piedmont, CVE and Reintegration Initiative, 29 April 2016.

48 Bourne and Greene, note 41 above, p. 199.

49 Paul Collier and Anke Hoeffler, "Murder by numbers: Socio-economic determinants of homicide and civil war", Centre for the Study of African Economies Working Paper 10, CSAE, Oxford, 2004.

50 Astri Suhrke, "The peace in between", in Astri Suhrke and Mats Berdal (eds), *The Peace in Between: Post-War Violence and Peacebuilding* (New York: Routledge: 2011), p. 18.

51 Powell, note 3 above, pp. 32–33.

52 DFID, *Understanding and Supporting Security Sector Reform* (London: DFID, 2002), p. 35.

53 Joseph di Chiaro III, *Reasonable Measures: Addressing the Excessive Accumulation and Unlawful Use of Small Arms* (Bonn: BICC, 1998), p. 22.

54 Kreutz et al., note 39 above, p. 73.

55 Boubacar N'Diaye, "The Central African Republic", in Alan Bryden and Vincenza Scherrer (eds), *Disarmament, Demobilization and Reintegration and Security Sector Reform: Insights from UN Experience in Afghanistan, Burundi, the Central African Republic and the Democratic Republic of the Congo* (Berlin: LIT Verlag, 2012), pp. 115–142 at p. 122.

56 Jane Chanaa, *Security Sector Reform: Issues, Challenges and Prospects* (New York: Oxford University Press, 2002), p. 18.

57 Bourne and Greene, note 41 above, pp. 187–188.

58 OECD-DAC, *Security System Reform and Governance: Policy and Good Practice* (Paris: OECD, 2004),p. 39.

59 The UN Integrated Disarmament, Demobilization and Reintegration Standards (IDDRS) was introduced in 2006 and contains a comprehensive set of policies and guidelines for UN support to DDR. It consolidates policy guidance drawn from the experience of UN departments, agencies, funds and programmes involved in DDR.

60 United Nations, note 1 above, Level 6.10, p. 15.

61 Ibid., p. 16.

62 OECD-DAC, note 7 above, p. 100.

63 UK Government, "Security sector reform strategy", GCPP SSR Strategy 2004–2005, London, 2004.

64 United Nations, note 1 above, Level 4.11, pp. 22–23.

65 EU Programme for Preventing and Combating Illicit Trafficking in Conventional Arms, 2001, http://fas.org/asmp/campaigns/smallarms/euprogram.htm.

66 Small Arms Survey, "State security forces", www.smallarmssurvey.org/armed-actors/state-security-forces.html.

67 Bourne and Greene, note 41 above, pp. 192–193.

68 Adedji Ebo, "Combating small arms proliferation and misuse after conflict", in Alan Bryden and Heiner Hänggi (eds), *Security Governance in Post-Conflict Peacebuilding* (Geneva: DCAF, 2005), pp. 137–158 at p. 152.

69 Bourne and Greene, note 41 above, p. 201.

70 United Nations, "Programme of Action to Prevent, Combat and Eradicate the Illicit Trade in Small Arms and Light Weapons in All Its Aspects", 2001, Sec III, Art. 6, www.poa-iss.org/PoA/poahtml.aspx.

71 Ibid.

72 "Co-ordinated agenda for action on the problem of the proliferation of small arms and light weapons in the Great Lakes region and the Horn of Africa", 2000, Sec. 4.2, www.issafrica.org/armsnetafrica/sites/default/files/saafo5.pdf.

73 Ibid., Sec. 4.7.

74 Thokozani Thusi, "Assessing small arms control initiatives in East Africa: The Nairobi Declaration", *African Security Review*, 12(2), 2003, p. 22.

75 See UN Programme of Action on Small Arms and Light Weapons, "Regional organizations", 2014, www.poa-iss.org/RegionalOrganizations/8.aspx.

76 Alex Vines, "Combating light weapons proliferation in West Africa", *International Affairs*, 81(2), 2005, pp. 341–360 at pp. 343–344.

77 Alhaji M. S. Bah, "Micro-disarmament in West Africa: The ECOWAS Moratorium on Small Arms and Light Weapons", *African Security Review*, 13(3), 2004, p. 42.

78 Ibid.

79 Vines, note 76 above, p. 359.

80 See Small Arms Survey, "Economic Community of West African States (ECOWAS)", 22 March 2012, www.smallarmssurvey.org/?id=943.

81 See UN Programme of Action on Small Arms and Light Weapons, "Economic Community of West African States (ECOWAS)", 2014, www.poa-iss.org/RegionalOrganizations/7.aspx; Linda Darkwa, "The challenge of sub-regional security in West Africa: The case of the 2006 ECOWAS Convention on Small Arms and Light Weapons", Nordic Africa Institute Discussion Paper, Nordiska Afrikainstitutet, Uppsala, 2011.

82 Bamako Declaration on an African Common Position on the Illicit Proliferation, Circulation and Trafficking of Small Arms and Light Weapons, 2000, Sec. 3, Art. ii, http://2001-2009.state.gov/t/ac/csbm/rd/6691.htm.

83 Ibid., Sec. 3, Art. iii.

84 Protocol on the Control of Firearms, Ammunition, and Other Related Materials in the Southern African Development Community (SADC) Region, 2001, Art. 6, www.sadc.int/files/8613/5292/8361/Protocol_on_the_Control_of_Firearms_Ammunition2001.pdf.

85 Ibid.

86 See Thusi, note 74 above, p. 26; Bah, note 77 above, p. 44.

87 Central African Convention for the Control of Small Arms and Light Weapons, Their Ammunition, Parts and Components that Can Be Used for Their Manufacture, Repair or Assembly, 2011, p. 3, www.poa-iss.org/revcon2/Documents/PrepCom-Background/Regional/ECCAS_Kinshasa%20Convention.pdf.

88 Ibid., p. 10

89 Ibid., pp. 18–19.

90 Ibid., p. 19.

91 Ibid., p. 23.

92 Ibid., p. 28.

93 African Union, "AU Strategy on the Control of Illicit Proliferation, Circulation and Trafficking of Small Arms and Light Weapons", 2011, http://unrec.org/docs/Strategy%20Final.pdf.

94 The members of the AU Regions Steering Committee on Small Arms are the Economic Community of Central African States, the Community of Sahel-Saharan States, the Common Market for Eastern and Southern Africa, the East African Community, ECOWAS, the Intergovernmental Authority on Development, the International Conference on the Great Lakes Region, the Regional Centre on Small Arms, the SADC and the Arab Maghreb Union. The EU and the UN Regional Centre for Peace and Disarmament in Africa serve as observers. See www.smallarmssurvey.org/?id=911.

95 See Small Arms Survey, "African Union (AU)", 2 June 2012, www.smallarmssurvey.org/?id=911.

96 UN Office for Disarmament Affairs, "The Arms Trade Treaty", 24 December 2014, www.un.org/disarmament/ATT/.

97 United Nations, "The Arms Trade Treaty", Res. 67/234B, Art. 16, No. 1, entered into force 24 December 2014, https://unoda-web.s3-accelerate.amazonaws.com/wp-content/uploads/2013/06/English7.pdf.

98 Centre for Humanitarian Dialogue, *Missing Pieces: A Guide for Reducing Gun Violence Through Parliamentary Action*, Handbook for Parliamentarians No. 12 (Geneva: Centre for Humanitarian Dialogue, 2007), p. 132.

99 United Nations, "Small arms", report of the Secretary-General, 22 August 2013, UN Doc. S/2013/503, p. 13.

100 OECD-DAC, note 7 above.

101 United Nations, note 99 above, p. 16.

102 Small Arms Survey, "Estimating law enforcement firearms", Small Arms Survey Research Notes No. 24, Geneva, 2012, p. 1.

103 OECD-DAC, note 7 above, p. 106

104 Ibid., p. 106.

105 Bourne and Greene, note 41 above, p. 199.

106 Personal communication with Dean Piedmont, CVE and Reintegration Initiative, 29 April 2016.

107 See Peter Dahl Thruelsen, *Security Sector Stabilisation in a Non-Permissive Environment* (Copenhagen: Royal Danish Defence College, 2010).

108 See Nat J. Colletta and Robert Muggah, "Context matters: Interim stabilization and second generation approaches to security promotion", *Conflict, Security & Development*, 9(4), 2009, pp. 425–453.

109 OECD-DAC, note 7 above, p. 106.

110 Ibid.

111 United Nations, "Integrated Disarmament, Demobilization and Reintegration Standards (IDDRS)", 2009, pp. 7–8, http://unddr.org/uploads/documents/IDDRS%206.10%20 DDR%20and%20SSR.pdf.

112 Atsushi Yasutomi, "Linking DDR and SSR in post-conflict states: Agendas for effective security sector reintegration", *Central European Journal of International and Security Studies*, 2(1), 2008.

113 United Nations, "Small arms and light weapons", UN Resolution 2117 (2013), UN Doc. S/RES/2117, 26 September 2013.

114 United Nations, note 99 above, p. 4.

115 Mark Bromley, Lawrence Dermody, Hugh Griffiths, Paul Holtom and Michael Jenks, "Transfers of small arms and light weapons to fragile states: Strengthening oversight and control", *SIPRI Insights on Peace and Security*, 1, 2013, pp. 1–20 at p. 13, http://books.sipri. org/files/insight/SIPRIInsight1301.pdf.

116 United Nations, note 99 above, p. 4.

117 OECD-DAC, note 7 above, pp. 106–107.

118 United Nations, note 111 above, p. 7.

119 N'Diaye, note 55 above, p. 122.

120 Centre for International Governance Innovation, "Southern Sudan", *Security Sector Reform Monitor*, No. 2, CIGI, Waterloo, ON, April 2010, p. 5.

121 OECD-DAC, note 7 above, pp. 106–107.

122 Launched in 2012, the International Small Arms Control Standards "provide clear, practical guidance to practitioners and policymakers on fundamental aspects of small arms and light weapons control". The standards have been put to a variety of uses, including supporting weapons assessments and surveys in post-conflict and fragile states; developing standard operating procedures, technical guides and training curricula for use at the national level; evaluating (and revising) the design of national small arms

control programmes; and providing consistent, high-quality advice to member states on fundamental aspects of SALW control. United Nations, "International Small Arms Control Standards 2012–13 activity report", 2012, p. 16.

123 United Nations, note 99 above, p. 5.

124 United Nations, "Assistance to states for curbing the illicit traffic in small arms and light weapons and collecting them: The illicit trade in small arms and light weapons in all its aspects", report of the Secretary-General, July 2013, UN Doc. A/68/171, p. 9.

125 Ibid.

126 United Nations, note 113 above.

127 Ibid.

128 United Nations, note 124 above, pp. 6–7.

129 Bromley et al., note 115 above, p. 3.

130 Ibid.

131 Ibid., p. 16.

132 Ibid.

133 Donald and Olonisakin, note 2 above.

134 Owen Greene and Elizabeth Kirkham, *Biting the Bullet – Preventing Diversion of Small Arms and Light Weapons: Strengthening Border Management Under the UN Programme of Action* (London: Saferworld, 2010), p. 6.

135 Karp, note 9 above, p. 165.

136 Greene and Kirkham, note 134 above, p. 6.

137 Ibid.

138 Ibid.

139 United Nations, *International Small Arms Control Standards: Border Controls and Law Enforcement Cooperation* (New York: United Nations, 2012), p. vi.

140 UNDP, *How-to Guide: Small Arms and Light Weapons Legislation* (New York: UNDP, 2008), p. 8.

141 OECD-DAC, note 7 above, p. 213.

142 UNDP, note 140 above, p. 8.

143 United Nations, note 111 above, p. ii.

144 Siobhan O'Neil and James Cockayne, "Introduction", in James Cockayne and Siobhan O'Neil (eds), *UN DDR in an Era of Violent Extremism: Is It Fit for Purpose?* (Tokyo: United Nations University, 2015), p. 25.

145 Karp, note 9 above, p. 180.

146 Muggah and O'Donnell, note 33 above.

147 O'Neil and Cockayne, note 144 above, p. 25.

148 UN DPKO, "Disarmament, demobilization and reintegration", www.un.org/en/peacekeeping/issues/ddr.shtml.

149 Muggah and O'Donnell, note 33 above.

150 Bourne and Greene, note 41 above, p. 203.

151 A 2007 report which surveyed 19 DDR programmes that were launched or completed in 2006 found they had an average duration of 3.5 years. See Escola de Cultura de Pau, "Analysis of DDR programmes in the world during 2006", 2007, http://escolapau.uab.cat/img/programas/desarme/ddr004i.pdf.

152 See Muggah and O'Donnell, note 33 above.

153 Personal communication with senior UN official, 17 February 2016.

154 See Eva Gross, "Assessing the EU's approach to security sector reform (SSR)", European Parliament Directorate-General for External Policies, Policy Department, 2013, www.europarl.europa.eu/RegData/etudes/etudes/join/2013/433837/EXPO-SEDE_ET(2013)433837_EN.pdf.

155 United Nations, "UN Inter-Agency SSR Task Force", http://unssr.unlb.org/TaskForceMembers/TaskForce.aspx.

156 Gregory Mthembu-Salter, *Trading Life, Trading Death: The Flow of Small Arms from Mozambique to Malawi* (Geneva: Small Arms Survey, 2009).

157 As one report noted, even if the institutions responsible for controlling the border were adequately staffed, the borders would remain "extremely porous" based on the country's geography. Christopher J. Pearce and Ulrich Weyl, "Rapid assessment of the small arms situation in Malawi", DECOSAC and GTZ, Eschborn, October–November 2002, p. 10.

158 Government of Malawi, "National progress report on the implementation of the UN Programme of Action to Prevent, Combat and Eradicate the Illicit Trade in Small Arms and Light Weapons in All Aspects", Fourth Biennial Meeting of States, June 2010, p. 2.

159 Saferworld, *Community Policing and Small Arms Control in Malawi* (London: Saferworld, 2001).

160 Government of Malawi, "Malawi Police Service: Strategic Development Plan, 1st July 2011–30th June 2016", 2011, www.apcof.org/files/1572_Malawi%20Police%20Strategic%20Plan%202011-2016.pdf.

161 Pearce and Weyl, note 157 above, p. 2.

162 Saferworld, note 159 above, p. 3.

163 Government of Malawi, note 158 above, p. 2.

164 Mthembu-Salter, note 156 above.

165 Pearce and Weyl, note 157 above.

166 Mike Brogden, "'Horses for courses' and 'thin blue lines': Community policing in transitional society", *Police Quarterly*, 8, 2005, p. 64.

167 Ibid.

168 Pearce and Weyl, note 157 above.

169 Ibid., p. 40.

170 Saferworld, note 159 above, p. 3.

171 Undule Mwakasungula and David Nungu, "Country study: Malawi", in Chandré Gould and Guy Lamb (eds), *Hide and Seek: Taking Account of Small Arms in Southern Africa*, Institute for Security Studies, 2004, www.issafrica.org/pubs/Books/Hide+Seek/Contents.htm.

172 Saferworld, note 159 above, p. 3.

173 Mwakasungula and Nungu, note 171 above.

174 Saferworld, note 159 above, p. 3.

175 Ibid.

176 Pearce and Weyl, note 157 above.

177 Lauren Hutton and Shiv Bakhrania, "GFN-SSR regional guide: Security sector reform in Southern Africa", GFN-SSR, Birmingham, 2010.

178 Ibid.

179 Sarah Parker and Katherine Green, "A decade of implementing the United Nations Programme of Action on Small Arms and Light Weapons: Analysis of national reports", UN Institute for Disarmament Research, 2012, www.unidir.org/files/publications/pdfs/a-decade-of-implementing-the-unpoa-analysis-of-national-reports-en-301.pdf.

180 Sarah Parker, "National implementation of the United Nations Small Arms Programme of Action and the international tracing instrument: An analysis of reporting in 2009–10", Small Arms Survey, Geneva, 2010, www.poa-iss.org/mge/Documents/Index/SAS-AnalysisofReporting.pdf.

181 Malawi Human Rights Commission, "Mid-term progress report: On the implementation of the United Nations Human Rights Council's universal periodic review recommendations to Malawi", 2013, www.hrcmalawi.org/midtermreport.pdf.

182 Government of Malawi, note 160 above.

183 Small Arms Survey, "Handgun ownership and armed violence in the Western Balkans", Issue Brief No. 4, Small Arms Survey, Geneva, September 2014, p. 3.

184 Sami Faltas and Wolf-Christian Paes, *You Have Removed the Devil from Our Door: An Assessment of the UNDP Small Arms and Light Weapons Control (SALWC) Project in Albania* (Tirana: SEESAC UNDP, 2003), p. 6.

185 Centre for Peace and Disarmament Education and Saferworld, *Turning the Page: Small Arms and Light Weapons in Albania* (London: Saferworld, 2005), p. 109.

186 Faltas and Paes, note 184 above, p. 6.

187 Collection teams were composed of 250 members, predominantly police officers and former military personnel, who were recruited due to their experience with handling weapons and ammunition. Centre for Peace and Disarmament Education and Saferworld, note 185 above, p. 108.

188 Ibid.; Small Arms Survey, note 183 above, p. 3.

189 Centre for Peace and Disarmament Education and Saferworld, note 185 above, p. 11.

190 Mariola Qesaraku and Besnik Baka, "Security sector reform in Albania: Challenges and failures since the collapse of communism", in Institute for European Policy, *Democracy Delayed: Obstacles in Political Transition*, 2011, p. 11, http://idmalbania.org/wp-content/uploads/2015/03/Security-sector-reform-in-Albania-Challenges-and-Failures-Since-the-Collapse-of-Communism.pdf.

191 Netherlands Ministry of Defence, "Multinational Advisory Police Element (MAPE) and the European Commission Police Assistance in Albania (ECPA)", undated, https://www.defensie.nl/english/topics/historical-missions/contents/mission-overview/1997/multinational-advisory-police-element-mape-and-the-european-commission-police-assistance-in-albania-ecpa.

192 Centre for Peace and Disarmament Education and Saferworld, note 185 above, p. 11.

193 European Union, "Consolidation of law enforcement capacities in Albania – PAMECA IV", http://pameca.org.al.

194 US Department of Justice, "International Criminal Investigative Training Assistance Program (ICITAP)", https://www.justice.gov/criminal-icitap.

195 Centre for Peace and Disarmament Education and Saferworld, note 185 above, p. 11.

196 Organization for Security and Co-operation in Europe (OSCE), "Report to the Permanent Council by the head of the OSCE Presence in Albania", 31 October 2013, p. 1, www.osce.org/albania/107715?download=true.

197 Ibid., p. 5.

198 Edward Laurance, "The UNDP role in the comprehensive approach to security in fragile states: An assessment", 10 June 2010, p. 4, www.miis.edu/media/view/21316/original/iccr.pdf.

199 Ibid.; Faltas and Paes, note 184 above, p. 4.

200 Geoffrey Mugumya, *From Exchanging Weapons for Development to Security Sector Reform in Albania: Gaps and Grey Areas in Weapon Collection Programmes Assessed by Local People* (Geneva: UNIDIR, 2004).

201 Centre for Peace and Disarmament Education and Saferworld, note 185 above, p. 111.

202 Faltas and Paes, note 184 above, p. 30.

203 Laurance, note 198 above, p. 5.

204 Faltas and Paes, note 184 above, p. 30.

205 Centre for Peace and Disarmament Education and Saferworld, note 185 above, p. 111.

206 Faltas and Paes, note 184 above, p. 28.

207 Ibid., p. 6.

208 Ibid., p. 30.

209 Centre for Peace and Disarmament Education and Saferworld, note 185 above, p. 118.

210 Ibid., p. 120

211 Ibid.

212 Barry J. Ryan, *An Evaluation of the UNDP's Support to Security Sector Reform in the Republic of Albania* (New York: UNDP, 2006).

213 Sean DeBlieck, *Monitoring and Evaluation Arrangements for the Support to Security Sector Reform Programme in Albania: A Case Study* (London: Saferworld, 2009), p. 1.

214 Ryan, note 212 above, p. 2.

215 DeBlieck, note 213 above.

216 DCAF, "Workshop report: Workshop on security sector reform: Institutional approaches", DCAF, Geneva, 2004, p. 2.

217 For instance, Ryan, note 212 above.

218 For instance, De Blieck, note 213 above; Enika Abazi, Aldo Bumci, Enri Hide and Albert Rakipi, *Security Sector Reform in Albania* (Brussels: Initiative for Peacebuilding, 2009).

219 Abazi et al., ibid., p. 18.

220 Victoria Walker, Ana Kantor, Everett Summerfield, Besnik Ahmeti and Sabina Ymeri, "Narrative report: SIDA project to support to community policing in Albania", DCAF, Geneva, 2010, pp. 10–11.

221 See SIDA, "Support to the MOI/ASP on community policing", 2011, http://issat.dcaf.ch/content/download/36982/545262/file/4.%20Sida-Final-MoI-Programme-Document%20-%20public%20version.pdf.

222 As one report wrote of the SIDA–MOI partnership, "throughout the whole design process, there has been clear evidence of enthusiasm and a desire to ensure success under Albanian leadership from the MoI, ASP and all other participants". Ibid., p. 1.

223 Peter Bartu and Neil Wilford, "Transitional justice and DDR: The case of Cambodia", International Centre for Transitional Justice, 2009, p. 22, https://www.ictj.org/sites/default/files/ICTJ-DDR-Cambodia-CaseStudy-2009-English.pdf.

224 David de Beer, *Small Arms Control in Cambodia: Lessons Learned from the EU ASAC Programme* (Eschborn: GTZ, 2005), p. 1.

225 Ibid.

226 Ibid.

227 Dylan Hendrickson, "Security sector reform and poverty alleviation: Options for DFID programming in Cambodia", CDSG Policy Studies No. 1, King's College, London, 1999, p. 2, http://www.securityanddevelopment.org/www.securityanddevelopment.org/pdf/CSDG%20Policy%20Studies%201.pdf.

228 Sami Faltas, Glenn McDonald and Camilla Waszink, "Removing small arms from society: A review of weapons collection and destruction programmes", Small Arms Survey, 2001, www.smallarmssurvey.org/fileadmin/docs/B-Occasional-papers/SAS-OP02-Weapons-Collection.pdf.

229 Dylan Hendrickson, "Cambodia's security-sector reforms: Limits of a downsizing strategy", *Journal of Conflict, Security and Development*, 1(1), pp. 67–82.

230 Ibid.

231 See, for instance, ibid.

232 EU-ASAC, "Project description: Weapons for development 2003", p. 2, www.eu-asac.org/programme/vwc/projectDescription.pdf.

233 EU-ASAC was described as consisting of four interrelated elements: "public awareness, voluntary hand in of weapons, police support and development incentives". See ibid., p. 6.

234 Gemma Kentaro, "Progress report on 'Peace Building and Comprehensive Small Arms Management Program in Cambodia'", JSAC, Phnom Penh, 2004, p. 3, www.bigpond.com.kh/users/adm.jsac/Reports%20Speeches/Progress%20Report%206-2004.pdf.

235 De Beer, note 224 above, p. 5.

236 Ibid., p. 6.

237 Ibid., p. 7.

238 Aaron Karp (ed.), *The Politics of Destroying Surplus Small Arms: Inconspicuous Disarmament* (London: Routledge, 2009).

239 JSAC, "Weapons Reduction and Development for Peace (WDP) Project", 2005, www.jics.or.jp/jsac/wdppjtEN.html.

240 Tiphaine Ferry, "How disarmament, demobilization and reintegration programs could have facilitated the establishment of long-term conflict prevention in post-conflict Cambodia", *Cambodia Law and Policy Journal*, 3, December 2014, p. 141.

241 JSAC, "Project achievements", 2008, www.jics.or.jp/jsac/jissekiEN.html.

242 Bartu and Wilford, note 223 above, p. 22; Ferry, note 240 above, p. 141.

243 Karp, note 238 above.

244 SEESAC, "Evaluation of the EU Small Arms and Light Weapons Assistance to the Kingdom of Cambodia (EU-ASAC)", EU, Brussels, 2006, www.seesac.org/res/files/publication/531.pdf.

245 EU-ASAC, "Voluntary weapons collection from the civil population", www.eu-asac.org/programme/weapons_collection.php.

246 De Beer, note 224 above, p. 9.

247 SEESAC, note 244 above, p. 19.

248 De Beer, note 224 above.

249 EU-ASAC, "Cambodian National Police training manual", www.eu-asac.org/programme/weapons_collection.php.

250 De Beer, note 224 above; SEESAC, note 244 above; Christina Wille, "Stabilizing Cambodia: Small arms control and security sector reform", in *Small Arms Survey 2006: Unfinished Business* (Geneva: Small Arms Survey, 2006), www.smallarmssurvey.org/fileadmin/docs/A-Yearbook/2006/en/Small-Arms-Survey-2006-Chapter-05-EN.pdf.

251 JSAC, "Recent activities", www.jics.or.jp/jsac/newsEN.html.

252 Ibid.

253 Ibid.

254 JSAC, "Safe Storage and Registration Project", 2005, www.jics.or.jp/jsac/SSpjtEN.html.

255 Mike Bourne and Owen Greene, *Armed Violence, Governance, Security Sector Reform and Safety, Security and Access to Justice* (Bradford: CICS, 2004).

256 Wille, note 250 above, p. 134

257 EU-ASAC, "Registration and safe storage", www.eu-asac.org/programme/photo_gallery.php?p=reg&page=1&photo=116.

258 JSAC, note 254 above.

259 Bourne and Greene, note 255 above.

260 Ibid.

261 Wille, note 250 above, p. 131.

262 Ibid.

263 De Beer, note 224 above, p. 9.

264 Bartu and Wilford, note 223 above, p. 23.

265 Vannarith Chheang, "Cambodian security and defence policy", in *Security Outlook of the Asia Pacific Countries and Its Implications for the Defence Sector* (Tokyo: National Institute for Defence Studies, 2013), p. 10, www.nids.go.jp/english/publication/asia_pacific/pdf/01.pdf.

266 Ferry, note 240 above, p. 152.

267 Edward Laurence and William H. Godnick, "Weapons collection in Central America: El Salvador and Guatemala", Bonn International Center for Conversion, January 2000, p. 3, http://sites.miis.edu/sand/files/2011/02/bicc_elsgua.pdf.

268 Ibid.

269 Nicholas Rosen and William H. Godnick, "BCPR – Strategic review – El Salvador", September 2005, p. 2, https://erc.undp.org/evaluation/documents/download/293.

270 Ibid., p. 3.

271 Ibid.

272 Ibid.

273 Ibid.

274 Salvador Samayoa, former FMLN senior negotiator, quoted in Cate Buchanan and Joaquín Chávez, "Negotiating disarmament: Guns and violence in the El Salvador peace negotiations", GSDRC, University of Birmingham, 2008, www.gsdrc.org/go/display&type=Document&id=4944.

275 Faltas et al., note 228 above, p. 10.

276 Ibid.

277 Ibid.

278 Buchanan and Chávez, note 274 above.

279 Faltas et al., note 228 above, p. 11.

280 Rosen and Godnick, note 269 above, p. 2.

281 UNDP, "El Salvador: An early example of peacebuilding", www.undp.org/content/undp/en/home/ourwork/crisispreventionandrecovery/projects_initiatives/el-salvador--an-early-example-of-peacebuilding.html.

282 Paola LeRoy, "Violence and poverty entangled in El Salvador", *Peace and Conflict Monitor*, 2012, www.monitor.upeace.org/archive.cfm?id_article=896.

283 Faltas et al., note 228 above, p. 10.

284 DCAF Community of Practice, "Country profile: El Salvador", 13 January 2015, http://issat.dcaf.ch/Home/Community-of-Practice/Resource-Library/Country-Profiles/El-Salvador-Country-Profile.

285 Douglas Farah, "The transformation of El Salvador's gangs into political actors", CSIS, 2012, http://csis.org/files/publication/120621_Farah_Gangs_HemFocus.pdf.

286 Ricardo Córdoba Macías, "Demilitarizing and democratizing Salvadoran politics", in Margarita S. Studemeister (ed.), *El Salvador: Implementation of the Peace Accords* (Washington, DC: US Institute of Peace, 2001), p. 27, www.usip.org/sites/default/files/pwks38.pdf.

287 Ibid.; Michael Shifter and Rachel Schwartz, "Democracy in progress: El Salvador's unfinished transition", *World Politics Review*, 2012, www.worldpoliticsreview.com/articles/12369/democracy-in-progress-el-salvadors-unfinished-transition.

288 LeRoy, note 282 above.

289 Laurance and Godnick, note 267 above, p. 15.

290 Laurance, note 198 above, p. 18.

291 Ibid.

292 Laurance and Godnick, note 267 above, p. 15.

293 Kimberly Slaby, "Security sector reform in Central America: Is it working?", 2003, http://sites.miis.edu/sand/files/2011/07/Security-Sector-Reform-in-Central-America-is-it-Working-Kimberly-Slaby.pdf.

294 UNDP, note 281 above.

295 Shifter and Schwartz, note 287 above.

296 Ibid.

297 DCAF Community of Practice, note 284 above.

298 Claire Ribando Seelke, "El Salvador: Background and U.S. relations", Congressional Research Service, 2016, p. 9, https://www.fas.org/sgp/crs/row/R43616.pdf.

299 See, for instance, Hannah Stone, "The Iron Fist returns to El Salvador", *InsightCrime*, February 2012, www.insightcrime.org/news-analysis/the-iron-fist-returns-to-el-salvador.

300 LeRoy, note 282 above.

301 DCAF Community of Practice, note 284 above.

302 Ibid.

303 Shifter and Schwartz, note 287 above.

304 UN Office on Drugs and Crime, "Transnational organized crime in Central America and the Caribbean: A threat assessment", 2012, www.unodc.org/documents/data-and-analysis/Studies/TOC_Central_America_and_the_Caribbean_english.pdf.

305 Hector Silva, "Violence and risky responses in El Salvador," AULA blog, 23 April 2015, http://aulablog.net/2015/04/23/violence-and-risky-responses-in-el-salvador/.

306 Seelke, note 298 above, p. 10.

307 Pew Research Center, "Mexicans and Salvadorans have positive picture of life in U.S., widespread concern about drugs and gangs at home", 24 October 2013, www.pewglobal.org/files/2013/10/Pew-Research-Center-Global-Attitudes-Mexico-El-Salvador-Report-FINAL-October-24-2013.pdf.

308 UN Office on Drugs and Crime, note 304 above.

309 G. Berghezan and X. Zeebroek, "Small arms in eastern Congo: A survey on the perception of insecurity", *Les Livres du GRIP*, 2011, http://archive.grip.org/en/siteweb/images/LIVRES_DU_GRIP/Small%20Arms%20in%20Eastern%20Congo.pdf.

310 Ibid.; UNHCR, "2015 UNHCR country operations profile – Democratic Republic of the Congo", 2015, www.unhcr.org/pages/49e45c366.html.

311 Berghezan and Zeebroek, note 309 above; Open Society Institute, "The Democratic Republic of Congo: Taking a stand on security sector reform", 2012, www.refworld.org/docid/4fbcc7ef2.html.

312 Amnesty International, "'If you resist we'll shoot you': The Democratic Republic of the Congo and the case for an effective arms trade treaty", 2012, www.amnestyusa.org/sites/default/files/12-06-08_arms_to_drc_-_final.pdf; Berghezan and Zeebroek, note 309 above.

313 Berghezan and Zeebroek, note 309 above.

314 Ibid., p. 5.

315 Amnesty International, note 312 above, p. 5.

316 Ibid., p. 7.

317 Berghezan and Zeebroek, note 309 above, p. 31.

318 Amnesty International, note 312 above, p. 30.

319 Ibid., p. 16.

320 Ibid.; V. Scherrer, "The Democratic Republic of the Congo", in A. Bryden and V. Scherrer (eds), *Disarmament, Demobilization and Reintegration and Security Sector Reform: Insights from UN Experience in Afghanistan, Burundi, the Central African Republic and the Democratic Republic of Congo* (Geneva: DCAF, 2012), www.dcaf.ch/content/download/97066/.../DDR-SSR_edited_14.03.2012.pdf.

321 Amnesty International, note 312 above, p. 10.

322 Ibid.

323 World Bank, "The Multi-Country Demobilization and Reintegration Program final report: Overview of program achievements", 2010, p. 1, http://tdrp.net/mdrp/PDFs/MDRP_Final_Report.pdf.

324 R. Bezerra, A. Disch, A.-M. Essoungou and E. Mobekk, "Multi-Country Demobilization and Reintegration Program: End of program evaluation", 2010, http://tdrp.net/mdrp/PDFs/MDRP_ReportFinalScanteam.pdf.

325 Small Arms Survey, "Demobilization in the DRC: Armed groups and the role of organizational control", 2013, p. 5, www.smallarmssurvey.org/fileadmin/docs/G-Issue-briefs/SAS-AA-IB1-DDR-in-the-DRC.pdf.

326 Ibid., p. 6.

327 Ibid.; Bezerra et al., note 324 above; MDRP, "MDRP Democratic Republic of Congo activities at a glance", 2009, p. 11, http://tdrp.net/mdrp/drc_main.htm.

328 As of 1 July 2010, MONUC was renamed the UN Organization Stabilization Mission in the Democratic Republic of the Congo (MONUSCO).

329 Berghezan and Zeebroek, note 309 above, p. 47.

330 Ibid., p. 54.

331 H. Boshoff, "Completing the demobilisation, disarmament and reintegration process of armed groups in the Democratic Republic of Congo and the link to security sector reform of FARDC", 2010, p. 6, http://dspace.africaportal.org/jspui/bitstream/123456789/30998/1/23Nov2010.pdf?1.

332 Berghezan and Zeebroek, note 309 above, p. 45.

333 CNC-ALPC, "Plan d'action national de contrôle et de gestion des ALPC en RDC", 2011, www.reseau-rafal.org/sites/reseau-rafal.org/files/document/externes/Plan%20d'action%20national%20ALPC%202012-2016.pdf.

334 Nina Wilén, "A window of opportunity for reforms in the Congo's security sector?", SSR 2.0 Brief No. 2, Centre for Security Governance, Waterloo, ON, 2014, p. 5.

335 Kasper Hoffmann, *Eastern DR Congo (DRC): Security Provision in the Context of Continuous Conflict and Militarisation* (Zurich: ISN, 2015).

336 Ibid.

337 Scherrer, note 320 above; Boshoff, note 331 above.

338 Scherrer, ibid.

339 Ibid.

340 Fidel Bafilemba, Aaron Hall and Timo Muller, *Crafting a Viable DDR Strategy for Congo* (Washington, DC: Enough Project, 2014), p. 2.

341 Ibid.

342 The centres also provide psychological support, skills training and civic education.

343 Bafilemba et al., note 340 above, p. 3.

344 E. Kets and H. de Vries, "Limits to supporting security sector interventions in the DRC", 2014, https://www.issafrica.org/uploads/Paper257.pdf.

345 Panapress, "Lancement en RDC d'une opération 'vélo contre arme à feu'", 2005, www.panapress.com/Lancement-en-RDC-d-une-operation--velo-contre-arme-a-feu---12-730104-145-lang1-index.html.

346 APA, "L'ONG PAREC remet au gouvernement de la RDC 21.961 armes à feu et effets militaires", 2009, http://www.congoindependant.com/article.php?articleid=4706.

347 Radio Okapi, "Bukavu: L'ONG PAREC lance l'opération 'Arme contre 100 USD'", 2009, http://radiookapi.net/actualite/2009/09/04/bukavu-long-parec-lance-loperation-«-arme-contre-100-usd/.

348 Ibid.; APA, note 346 above.

349 B. Aluma, "50 dollars contre une arme de feu dans le Kivu", 2010, http://fr.allafrica.com/stories/201005130223.html; APA, note 346 above.

350 UNDP, "Lancement official du project de désarmement volontaire des civils en Ituri", 2014, www.cd.undp.org/content/rdc/fr/home/presscenter/pressreleases/2014/03/12/d-sarmement-communautaire-en-ituri/.

351 Radio Okapi, "Ituri: 11,000 armes récupérées auprès des civils", 2014, www.radiookapi.net/actualite/2014/08/08/ituri-11-000-armes-recuperees-aupres-des-civils.

352 UN Security Council, "Unanimously adopting Resolution 2198 (2015), Security Council renews arms embargo, related sanctions on Democratic Republic of Congo", press release, 29 January 2015, www.un.org/press/en/2015/sc11757.doc.htm.

353 Bromley et al., note 115 above.

354 UN Security Council, note 352 above.

355 Ibid.

356 CNC-ALPC, note 333 above.

357 Ibid.; Amnesty International, note 312 above, p. 14.

358 Afriquejet, "Marquage électronique d'armes en RD Congo", 2015, www.afriquejet.com/afrique-centrale/15750-marquage-electronique-d-armes-en-rd-congo.html.

359 Ibid.

360 Amnesty International, note 312 above; UN Security Council, note 352 above.

361 CNC-ALPC, note 333 above.

362 For a detailed discussion of the shortcomings of SSR programming in the DRC see ASADHO, Eastern Congo Initiative, APPG, Enough Project, Eurac, FIDH, Groupe Lotus, Ligue des Electeurs, OENZ, OSISA, Refugees International, Congolese Network for Security Sector Reform and Justice and Pole Institute, "The Democratic Republic of Congo: Taking a stand on security sector reform", 2012, https://www.opensocietyfoundations.org/sites/default/files/drc-ssr-report-20120416-1.pdf.

363 CNC-ALPC, note 333 above.

364 Ibid.

365 Ibid.

366 D. M. Tull, "Weak states and successful elites: Extraversion strategies in Africa", 2011, www.swp-berlin.org/fileadmin/contents/products/research_papers/2011_RP09_tll_ks.pdf.

367 Wilén, note 334 above, p. 4.

368 Islamic Republic of Afghanistan, *Millennium Development Goals Islamic Republic of Afghanistan Country Report 2005: Vision 2020* (Kabul: Islamic Republic of Afghanistan and UNDP, 2005), p. 108.

369 C. J. Chivers, "Small arms, big problems: The fallout of the global gun trade", *Foreign Affairs,* January/February 2011.

370 After almost three decades of war, Afghanistan is littered with weaponry – from 500,000 to 1.5 million small arms and light weapons, according to the Small Arms Survey – and a significant proportion of the male population are affiliated with non-state armed groups.

371 For a discussion of DDR and SSR programming in Afghanistan see Mark Sedra, "Afghanistan and the DDR-SSR nexus", in Melanne A. Civil and Michael Miklaucic (eds), *Monopoly of Force: The Nexus of DDR and SSR* (Washington, DC: NDU Press, 2011), pp. 249–264; Caroline A. Hartzell, "Missed opportunities: The impact of DDR on SSR in Afghanistan", USIP, Washington, DC, 2011, www.usip.org/sites/default/files/SR270-Missed_Opportunities.pdf.

372 Quoted in Mark Sedra, "Challenging the warlord culture: Security sector reform in Afghanistan", BICC Paper 25, Bonn, 2002, p. 3.

373 Afghanistan New Beginnings Programme, "Afghanistan New Beginnings Programme", brochure for second Tokyo Conference on Consolidation of Peace in Afghanistan, ANBP, Kabul, 15 June 2006.

374 Ibid., p. 2.

375 The Asia Foundation has been conducting public opinion polls in Afghanistan since 2004. In 2015 57.5 per cent of Afghans believed the country is moving in the wrong direction and 67.4 per cent feared for their personal safety, both of which are the highest figures since the surveys began. Asia Foundation, "Afghanistan in 2015: A survey of the Afghan people", November 2015, http://asiafoundation.org/resources/pdfs/Afghanistanin2015.pdf.

376 Mark Sedra, "An uncertain future for Afghanistan's security sector", *Stability: International Journal of Security and Development*, 3(1), 2014.

377 For a discussion of SSR "under fire" in Afghanistan see Andrew Mackay, Mark Sedra and Geoff Burt, "Security sector reform (SSR) in insecure environments: Learning from Afghanistan", *Journal of Security Sector Management*, 3(8), 2011.

378 Mark Sedra, interview with senior ANBP official, Kabul, 12 January 2009.

379 UNDP, "Afghanistan, Disbandment of Illegal Armed Groups (DIAG): Second quarter project progress report – 2009", UNDP, Kabul, 2009, p. 9.

380 UNDP, "Disbandment of Illegal Armed Groups (DIAG): Annual project report 2010", UNDP, Kabul, 2010, p. 3.

381 See, for instance, Heath Druzin, "Fearing post-2014 environment, Afghans buy up weapons", *Stars & Stripes*, 5 December 2012; Jaïr van der Lijn, "Afghanistan post-2014: Groping in the dark", Clingendael, May 2013, www.clingendael.nl/sites/default/files/Afghanistan%20post%202014%20Groping%20in%20the%20dark.pdf.

382 UNAMA, "Afghanistan – Annual report 2015: Protection of civilians in armed conflict", UNAMA, Kabul, February 2016.

383 Interview with Combined Security Transition Command – Afghanistan official in Kabul, 16 May 2005; Special Inspector General for Afghanistan Reconstruction, "Afghan National Security Forces: Actions needed to improve weapons accountability", SIGAR 14–84 Audit Report, Washington, DC, 2014; US Department of Defense Inspector General, "Assessment of U.S. and coalition efforts to develop the sufficiency of Afghan National Security Forces' policies, processes, and procedures for the management and

accountability of Class III (fuel) and V (ammunition)", Report No. DODIG-2015-108, US DoD, Washington, DC, 30 April 2015.

384 This includes weapons such as rifles, pistols, machine guns, grenade launchers and shotguns.

385 Special Inspector General for Afghanistan Reconstruction, note 383 above.

386 Ibid., p. 12.

387 Michael Vinay Bhatia and Mark Sedra, *Afghanistan, Arms and Conflict: Armed Groups, Disarmament and Security in a Post-War Society* (London: Routledge, 2007); Jonathan Broder and Sami Yousafzai, "Arming the enemy in Afghanistan", *Newsweek*, 18 May 2015.

388 Bhatia and Sedra, ibid.

389 Ibid.

390 Ibid.

391 Thousands of small arms flow unimpeded into Afghanistan from neighbouring countries each month, mostly from Pakistan and Iran. Cracking down on unlicensed weapons distribution in the tribal areas on both sides of the Afghan–Pakistan border through the strengthening of border control structures – something the Pakistani government has attempted to do in relation to the arms bazaars in the North West Frontier Province – represents a major opportunity for SSR–SALW integration. Mark Sedra, "Afghanistan", in Alan Bryden and Vincenza Scherrer (eds), *Disarmament, Demobilization and Reintegration and Security Sector Reform: Insights from UN Experience in Afghanistan, Burundi, the Central African Republic and the Democratic Republic of the Congo* (Geneva: DCAF, 2012), p. 49, www.isn.ethz.ch/Digital-Library/Publications/Detail/?id=152934.

392 Special Investigator General for Afghanistan Reconstruction, "Afghan Local Police: A critical rural security initiative lacks adequate logistics support, oversight, and direction", SIGAR 16-3 Audit Report, Washington, DC, October 2015.

393 US Department of Defense, *Enhancing Security and Stability in Afghanistan* (Washington, DC: US DoD, 2015), p. 73; Matthieu Aikins, "A US-backed militia runs amok in Afghanistan", *Al Jazeera America*, 23 July 2014.

394 Ibid.

395 Gopal Ratnam, "Afghan Minister Daudzai sees accord with U.S. on security", *Bloomberg*, 7 November 2013.

396 See, for instance, International Crisis Group, "The future of the Afghan Local Police", Asia Report No. 268, 2015, www.crisisgroup.org/~/media/Files/asia/south-asia/pakistan/268-the-future-of-the-afghan-local-police.pdf; Human Rights Watch, "Afghanistan: Don't expand Afghan Local Police", 2011, https://www.hrw.org/news/2011/12/15/afghanistan-dont-expand-afghan-local-police; Mujib Mashal, "Afghan plan to expand militia raises abuse concerns", *New York Times*, 16 October 2015, www.nytimes.com/2015/10/17/world/asia/afghan-local-police-taliban.html?_r=0; Kevin Sieff, "Afghans want end to US police training", *Financial Times*, 15 January 2013, www.ft.com/cms/s/0/9328f25e-5f2d-11e2-8250-00144feab49a.html#axzz4160BVqRx.

397 Presidential Decree 50, 14 July 2004.

398 Ibid.

399 Law of Fire Weapons, Ammunitions and Explosive Materials, Ch. 1, Art. 4.

400 Sedra, note 391 above, p. 49.

401 Islamic Republic of Afghanistan, note 368 above, p. 108.

402 Sedra, note 391 above, p. 50.

403 Draft Law on Private Security Organizations, Ch. 2, Art. 6.

404 Ibid., Ch. 3, Arts 8–9.
405 Sedra, note 391 above, p. 61.
406 United Nations, note 111 above, p. 5.
407 Ebo, note 68 above, p. 152.
408 Bourne and Greene, note 41 above, p. 206.
409 OECD-DAC, note 7 above, p. 105.
410 Ibid.
411 United Nations, note 111 above, p. 7.
412 Ibid., p. 16.
413 Ibid., p. 5.

www.ingramcontent.com/pod-product-compliance
Lightning Source LLC
Chambersburg PA
CBHW080305030726
47593CB00009B/2639